ISLAM AND CHRISTIANITY
AT THE CROSSROADS

For centuries, Christianity and Islam ha
Because both faiths disagree with each c
believers have often been tempted to cor
own faith with the worst of the other.

And yet, despite the real differences between them, Islam and
Christianity share common ground. They both claim to be
related to Abraham, the Father of the believers. They both
acknowledge God's greatest prophets such as Moses and
David. They both consider the Torah as the first Book where
God's Word is revealed. And, above all, they are both
characterized by an unshakeable belief in the oneness of God,
his majesty and his deep concern for mankind, the highest of
his creatures.

This book is a call for Christians and Muslims to understand
each other. It challenges them to reassess the common ground
they hold, and to face up honestly to the disagreements
between the two faiths. It aims at promoting a genuine
dialogue, in truth and love, between Christians and Muslims.

Chawkat Georges Moucarry was born into a Christian family
in Syria, where he had an Arab education. This book is the
result of many years of study in both Christianity and Islam, as
well as of experience in Christian-Muslim relationships.

ISLAM AND CHRISTIANITY

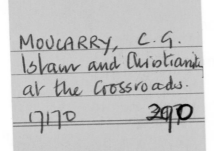

This edition copyright © 1988 Lion Publishing
Original edition copyright © 1984 Presses Bibliques Universitaires

Published by
Lion Publishing plc
Icknield Way, Tring, Herts, England
ISBN 0 7459 1276 1
Albatross Books Pty Ltd
PO Box 320, Sutherland, NSW 2232, Australia
ISBN 0 86760 929 X

First English edition 1988

Originally published 1984 under the title *La Foi en Questions* by Presses
Bibliques Universitaires, Switzerland

British Library Cataloguing in Publication Data

Moucarry, Chawkat Georges
   Islam and Christianity at the crossroads.
   1. Christianity and other religions—Islam
   2. Islam—Relations—Christianity
   I. Title   II. La Foi en questions. *English*
   261.2'7   BP172

   ISBN 0-7459-1276-1

Printed and bound in Great Britain by
Cox & Wyman, Reading

'This child [Jesus] is destined . . . to be a sign that
will be spoken against.'
New Testament, Luke 2:34

'He [Jesus] shall be a sign to mankind.'
Qur'an, sura 19 (Maryam):21

Notes to the reader

The English rendering of Arabic words found in this book follows the international system of transliteration, with some exceptions.

All Bible quotations are taken from the New International Version (Zondervan, 1978, USA and Hodder & Stoughton, 1979, UK). Unless otherwise stated, all Qur'an quotations are taken from *The Koran* (Penguin Books, 1956), translated by N. J. Dawood.

Dates mentioned in the text refer to the Christian Era (CE), unless otherwise indicated.

The following abbreviations are used in the notes at the end of each chapter: OT, Old Testament; NT, New Testament, and Q, Qur'an.

CONTENTS

FOREWORD

This book is not a theological treatise. That sort of book would involve very detailed argument, very technical language and many more pages! Rather, it is a personal statement by one who grew up on the borderline between Islam and Christianity. I was born into a Christian family in Syria. For me, as a young man, Islam was part of the life experience I shared with school friends, whom I remember with great affection. A few years later, when I went to live in France, I began to study Islam seriously. About ten years ago I discovered, through studying the Bible, what my life means in the light of faith in Jesus Christ.

This personal statement, therefore, springs from my Islamic and Christian roots. It is not neutral — if neutrality means not saying which side you agree with in a debate. On the other hand, if being 'objective' means faithfully reporting the facts of history and the thoughts of human beings, then this book has been written with a concern for objectivity. If it manages to clear up some misunderstandings, to question a few prevailing opinions and to define more clearly the relationship between Islam and Christianity, then it will not have been written in vain.

I would like to thank my theology teachers, both Christian and Muslim, and my friends of both faiths who have always stimulated my thinking about the various questions tackled in this book.

THE AUTHOR

1

ISLAM: AN ALTERNATIVE RELIGION?

In the sixth century of the Christian era most Arab people were living in the peninsula which is named after them — the Arabian Peninsula. They believed in God (Allah) but also in many other gods which were represented in the temple at Mecca. The Ka'ba was an all important centre of pilgrimage for all the inhabitants of the area. Belief in Fate and in the spirit world strongly influenced their worship, which was full of superstition.[1]

Several Jewish communities existed in Arabia, particularly in the city of Yaṯrib. Their Judaism was based on the Talmud and strongly influenced by the Apocrypha. Christianity was also present in that area. The Christians in the east were Nestorians, supported by the Sassanid Empire. In the north of the Peninsula were the Monophysites, vassals of the Byzantine Empire.[2] These two empires were by then exhausted by the successive wars which they had been waging against each other.[3]

Muhammad was born in Mecca about the year 570 CE. He was born into a world of political, social and religious turmoil. At the age of forty he began preaching the Qur'an in order to combat idolatry or polytheism (*širk*) among the Arabs. He wanted to convince them of the absolute authority of God and to persuade them to be subject to their Creator. According to Muhammad the Qur'an was simply an Arabic version of the Scripture already revealed to the Jews and the Christians.[4]

The Arabs could therefore no longer ignore the divine revelation.[5] Anxious to maintain the status quo, the tribal chiefs of Mecca refused to convert to Islam. This refusal raised doubts in the mind of Muhammad and the first Muslims about their new faith. The Qur'an, to assure them of its divine origin, referred them back to the Jews and to the Christians who would speak in its favour.[6]

In 622 Muhammad left Mecca, with his companions, to join the Arab tribes in Yaṭrib. It was then that the city was re-named Medina and became the home of the young Muslim community, which kept growing. So the prophetic message became more and more a social message, and Muhammad himself became a political, as much as a religious, leader. As a result, the dominant power of the Jewish community in Medina found itself challenged. In 624, the rift between the two communities came to a head with the changing of the Qiblah — the direction which Muslims face in prayer.[7] From that time on the Muslims turned towards Mecca, rather than towards Jerusalem when they prayed. Muhammad also began to criticize the Christians, particularly for their human representations of God.[8]

In 630 Muhammad did what he had always wanted, and led his army into Mecca. The city surrendered peacefully and the temple was purged of its idols. The Arabs now began to join the new religion in great numbers, recognizing its founder as their supreme leader. In 632 Muhammad led a pilgrimage to Mecca, in the course of which he announced to the Muslims that he had perfected their religion.[9] A few months later he died in Medina, leaving behind him a people whose unity, so recently achieved, had its roots deep in the absolute oneness of God.

THE MUSLIM COMMUNITY — HOLDING THE MIDDLE GROUND

Muhammad may justly be considered the founder of the Arab nation as well as of the Muslim community. Just as Muhammad had both a political and a religious role to play, so too does that Law of God in Islam: it is the foundation of the State as well as of the religion.

The Muslim community sees itself as avoiding extremes. Half-way between the Jewish and Christian communities, it carries on their monotheistic tradition. This Qur'anic idea of the 'middle ground' is shown in several ways. According to Muslim thinkers:

- On the one side there are the Jews, who refused to believe in Jesus as the Messiah. On the other there are the Christians, who claim that Jesus is the Son of God. In between are the Muslims, who recognize that Jesus is one of God's great prophets.
- The Jewish Law has hardly any concern for the after-life. Christian teaching, by contrast makes earthly sacrifices for the sake of heavenly blessings. The Muslim Law keeps the necessary balance between life on earth and the after-life.
- The Jewish community follows a code of criminal law which is too strict and a moral code which is not strict enough. The Christian community, on the other hand, follows a criminal code which is too lenient and a moral code which is too strict. The Muslim community keeps to the middle way: Muslims follow a code of law which is neither too hard nor too easy for them.[10] So Muslim law is the most perfect expression of God's will.

In Muhammad's day the Arabs thought of Judaism and Christianity as two foreign religions, each competing against the other to become the dominant faith. This presented the Arabs with a dilemma: either they must turn to one of these two religions, and so sacrifice their own identity as Arabs, or they must stay out in the spiritual wilderness. Islam appeared to offer them an alternative. It had strong links with the other two religions, but it raised their self-awareness as a nation and offered them a faith based on a book revealed in their own language.

ISLAM AS A NEW ALTERNATIVE TO A NEW DILEMMA

For many Muslims today Islam offers a new alternative to a new dilemma. Some Muslim countries, since achieving independence, have organized their political and economic life on capitalist lines, whereas others have adopted the socialist system. The capitalist system, generally associated with Western countries with a Christian tradition has led to materialism at the expense of human values. Capitalist societies have rushed headlong into industrial progress at the expense of individual human dignity, and into immorality and violence. The socialist system, generally associated with Communist, atheistic regimes, has often led to dictatorship, economic stagnation and religious oppression . . . The political regimes which have chosen these types of social organization have not kept all their promises, and so Islam appears once again as the alternative way, which can build a society of justice and progress on the religious heritage of the Islamic nations.

So today, as yesterday, Islam is put forward as a healthy alternative to other political systems in Muslim countries.

Perhaps non-Muslim people might also decide to choose this way of life? Why not? After all, some people in Western countries are being converted to Islam. However, the history of Christendom makes this seem unlikely. Ever since the reign of Constantine, through the period of the

Crusades and until quite recent times, whenever politics and religion have worked together, they have suppressed individual freedom to a greater or lesser extent. This partly explains why Islam was so successful soon after the death of Muhammad in countries such as Syria and Egypt which were originally Christian. Many Christians in these countries had not accepted the official teachings of their church, which was the church of the Byzantine Empire. They welcomed the arrival of the victorious Muslim armies, hoping that the Muslims would free them from the yoke of the Empire.

Because they believe in the oneness of God, Jews and Christians have special status within the Muslim community. The Qur'an expressly forbids Muslims to force anyone to convert to Islam.[11] That is why such harmonious relationships existed between Jews, Christians and Muslims at the height of the Muslim Empire's glory. But, in an age when religion is no longer an integral part of people's lives, it is questionable whether Islam can still be thought of as a State religion without it leading to dictatorship. The Qur'an teaches that monotheism is the only right religion for mankind. This means that non-monotheistic citizens of a Muslim state can hardly refuse to convert to Islam.[12]

Certainly, though, Islam has undergone some encouraging changes in recent decades. Nowadays, many Muslims emphasize, more than they used to, the close connection between the prophetic message and the historical context in which it arose. In this way they try to allow for the development of modern societies and the facts of modern social science. Two examples of this relatively recent shift in Islamic thinking are the abolition, in Tunisia in 1957, of the Qur'anic law permitting polygamy, and the PLO argument in favour of a democratic Palestinian state. On the other hand, in recent times we have also seen the political power of Islam increasing again, with the setting up of the Islamic Republic in Iran. There is thus a struggle between two opposite trends in contemporary Islam, and it looks as though the second of these — the revival of Islamic fundamentalism — may win the day unless we take seriously certain just claims of the Muslim peoples.

JESUS AND POLITICAL POWER

At the beginning of the Christian era, Palestine was part of the Roman Empire. Among the religious parties which were struggling to win the Jews' allegiance, there were the Zealots, who backed armed force against the Romans. By means of violent insurrections they had tried to drive out the occupying power, but these had all failed amid much bloodshed.[13]

It is in this troubled climate, when most Jews were looking for a liberator who would rise up from among them, that the Virgin Mary learns that she will be the mother of the Messiah, who will sit on the throne of David and whose reign will have no end.[14] Jesus' birth is greeted by wise men from the East who have come to worship the King of the Jews. King Herod, told of this by the wise men, seeks to kill the baby king. Jesus' parents have to flee to Egypt to escape Herod's murderous intent.[15]

Jesus begins his ministry by calling people to repent in order to enter the kingdom of God.[16] This will be a kingdom of humility, mercy, purity, justice and peace.[17] He identifies himself as the Messiah whose coming was foretold by the prophets,[18] but he refuses to take on the kingship that the crowds want to give him.[19] He teaches his disciples to love their enemies[20] and, following the example that he has given them, to be the servants of one another.[21] When his disciples recognize that he is the Messiah, he commands them immediately not to tell anyone of it, lest people should credit him with political kingship.[22] For his kingship would mean losing his life.[23]

As the moment for which he came into the world approaches, Jesus sets out for Jerusalem,[24] knowing that death awaits him at the end of the road.[25] He makes his messianic entry into Jerusalem, but knows full well the tragic fate awaiting him.[26] He publicly disclaims that he is a political Messiah[27] and does not hesitate to declare to the Jewish authorities, who were trying to catch him out so as to hand him over to the Roman governor, that one must give to Caesar that which is Caesar's and to God that which is God's.[28] At the moment of his arrest, he refuses to let his disciples use violence to defend him ('All who live by the sword will die by the sword'), and he sees his death as accomplishing the will of God as revealed in the Scriptures.[29] Before Pilate, the Roman governor, he claims that he is King of the Jews, although his kingdom is not of this world.[30] He also states that Pilate would have no power over him unless it had been given him from God.[31] Jesus then dies on a cross which bears the inscription 'Jesus of Nazareth, King of the Jews'.[32] But he rises from the dead and appears to two of his disciples, who had lost all hope of seeing their master liberate Israel from the crushing oppression of the Romans. He explains to them that the Scriptures showed that the Messiah *had* to suffer and die *before* entering into his glory.[33]

Jesus' resurrection demonstrates his victory over death, which is man's true enemy.[34] His ascension into heaven marks his enthronement at the right hand of God.[35] All those who confess that Jesus is Lord attest too that he is King of Kings, 'who is, and who was, and who is to come'[36] to judge all the nations and to establish his kingdom for ever.

THE STATE AND THE KINGDOM

Although Christians believe in the sovereign rule of God,

this does not mean that the state and the kingdom of God are one and the same thing.

The concept of the state is based on natural law,[37] the law written by God in the heart of every person. It is this which explains the ability of non-religious people to distinguish good from evil. Sin weakens this ability but does not destroy it. Because of the effect of sin in the world, it is important for Christians to be, in the words of Jesus, the light of the world and the salt of the earth.[38]

The kingdom of God is potentially here already, in the form of the church, but it will be set up for all to see only when Jesus Christ returns in glory. In the meantime the specific instruction to Christians is to witness to the kingdom of God and to preach the good news of the gospel which is the basis of the kingdom. For a person to become a member of this kingdom, he must decide, of his own free will, to believe in Jesus Christ. For a person to live according to the standards set by the gospel, he needs the power of God's Spirit, the only power which can transform him from within and set him free from sin.

This distinction between the state and the kingdom makes the law of the state clearly different from the gospel of the kingdom. The law of the state rewards those who do good and punishes those who do evil. The gospel of the kingdom is the good news of salvation — that people can be saved by God from the power of sin within their own human nature. Christians, by obeying God and doing what is right, aim to leave a mark on the world, a mark which will act as a sign announcing the coming kingdom.

The Western church has not generally maintained this clear distinction between the state and the kingdom. For this reason, Christianity has become discredited in the eyes of many people who have been led to think that Western civilization was the actual embodiment of the gospel. This is probably the greatest dis-service done by the church to the name of Christ in the Muslim world. In the longer term this abuse of power led to the eventual separation between church and state in some Western countries. Paradoxically, this separation is much more in line with the pattern of teaching we find in the New Testament. It is true, of course, that technological progress, democracy and the Declaration of Human Rights all have some connection with the positive influence of Christianity on Western civilization. However, it cannot be denied, and Muslims quite rightly point out, that Western civilization today is also characterized by the rise of atheistic humanism, a decline in moral standards and a certain dehumanization of the individual.

Christians who are inclined to look too favourably upon Western culture should bear these things in mind. They are not so much the price we have to pay for science, freedom and prosperity as they are the result of the departure from Western Judaeo-Christian values.

This situation requires Christians, especially in the West, to recognize their dual responsibility. In the first place they should repudiate, in a true spirit of repentance, the church's past errors; but that alone is not enough. They should also learn a lesson from the spirit of today's Islamic revival, and, by their complete faithfulness to the gospel, seek to express visibly the kingdom of God in our complex modern world.

NOTES

1   The name of Muhammad's father, '*Abd Allâh* 'servant of God', shows that God was the chief among the many gods worshipped by the Arabs in the pre-Islamic period.
2   Monophysites recognized only one nature in the person of

Jesus Christ. Nestorians, on the other hand, recognized two persons and two natures in Jesus Christ. The Council of Chalcedon in 451 confessed, in line with biblical revelation, the union of the human and divine natures in the unique person of Jesus Christ.

3   Three Arab tribes had embraced Judaism: the Banû Naḍir, the Banû Qurayẓa and the Banû Qaynuqâ'. The eastern Christians were the Banû Laḥm and those in the north were the Banû Ġassân. It is probably owing to the presence of these two religions in Arabia that God appeared in Arab religion, and it may explain why they called angels 'daughters of God'.

4   Q sura 16 (Al-Naḥl):103; sura 26 (Al-Shu'arâ'):195; sura 42 (Al-Shûra):7; sura 43 (Al-Zukhruf):3; sura 46 (Al-Aḥqâf):12.

5   Q sura 6 (Al-An'âm):155–57.

6   Q sura 10 (Yûnis):94; sura 16 (Al-Naḥl):43; sura 21 (Al-Anbiyâ'):7.

7   Two Jewish tribes were driven out of Medina in the year 624. In 627 the last tribe in the city was wiped out.

8   In 632 Muhammad received a delegation sent by the Christian community in Najrân. Realizing the points of disagreement between them, the two parties struck a bargain. The Christians agreed to pay tribute to the Muslims in return for which the Muslims agreed to guarantee protection for the Christians, their possessions and their religious life.

9   Q sura 5 (Al-Mâ'ida):3.

10 Q sura 22 (Al-Ḥajj):78.

11 Q sura 2 (Al-Baqara):256.

12 Q sura 9 (Al-Tawba):29.

13 NT Acts 5:36–37.

14 NT Luke 1:31–33.

15 NT Matthew 9:1–18.

16 NT Matthew 4:17.

17 NT Matthew 5:3–10.

18 NT Matthew 11:2–6; Luke 4:16–21.

19 NT John 6:5–15.

20 NT Matthew 18:21–35.

21 NT Luke 22:24–27; John 13:1–16.
22 NT Matthew 16:13–20.
23 NT Matthew 16:21.
24 NT Luke 9:51.
25 NT Luke 12:49–50.
26 NT Luke 19:41–44.
27 NT Matthew 22:41–45.
28 NT Luke 20:20–25.
29 NT Matthew 26:52–54.
30 NT John 18:33–37.
31 NT John 19:8–11.
32 NT John 19:19.
33 NT Luke 24:13–32.
34 NT 1 Corinthians 15:26, 55.
35 NT Acts 13:32–37.
36 NT Revelation 1:8.
37 NT Matthew 22:21; Romans 2:14–15; 13:1–7.
38 NT Matthew 5:13–14.

2
ISRAEL: GOD'S CHOSEN PEOPLE?

If the State of Israel had not been re-born in 1948, the question of Israel as God's chosen people would probably have remained a purely academic and theological issue in the debate between Christians and Muslims. As it is, the rebirth of Israel has made the question highly political, and given it an emotional and often dramatic intensity.

Recalling the promise made by God to Abraham and the 1,000 years of Israel's history in the Promised Land, Zionists take the view that this land belongs by right to the Jewish people. After long centuries of exile, the Jews have finally recovered their right to an independent state open to Jews from all over the world who wish to live with dignity in the land of their fathers. The West, conscious of the terrible treatment suffered by the Jews, particularly during the Second World War, supports the State of Israel, having played a decisive role in its creation.

The Palestinians, for their part, look back on more than 1,000 years during which the Palestinian people lived in this same land. They see their homeland taken from them by a sort of colonialist movement, Zionism, whose ideology is based on religious and racial criteria.

As innocent victims, suffering the consequences of the persecution of the Jews in Europe, the Palestinians claim the right to an independent state on their native soil in which Jews, Christians and Muslims can live on equal terms.

The Arabs, and Muslims generally, support the Palestinian cause and denounce the West's pro-Zionist policies which they see as designed to serve Western interests in this strategically important part of the world.

Western Christians are inevitably held partly responsible for this situation. There are even some among them who uphold certain Zionist claims, saying that the nation of Israel is God's chosen people and Palestine their Promised Land.

The purpose of this chapter is not to weigh up the rights of the two conflicting parties to set up an independent state in Palestine. But Christians cannot escape the questions presented to them by the problem of the Middle East. Nor can they remain indifferent to the dreadful crises confronting both peoples. This chapter will confine itself to examining the religious basis of Zionism, from a Christian viewpoint, and to suggesting a Christian approach to this tragic conflict.[1]

THE FIRST PROMISE

We read in the first two chapters of Genesis, in the Old Testament, that God, after creating Adam, made an agreement ('covenant') with him. This agreement, expressed in figurative language, offered to mankind abundant life and the whole of God's creation to enjoy. But it also warned us that if we made ourselves the supreme judge of good and evil, robbing God of his exclusive right, then certain death awaited us. Yielding to Satan's tempting, the first man and woman broke this agreement and thus set themselves firmly on the road towards death. From then on, every aspect of human life had the shadow of death hanging over it.

This 'fall' of mankind related in the third chapter of Genesis, did not take God by surprise! Nor did it put an end to his love for the human race. Immediately after man's sin, God made a solemn promise: that one day a descendant born of the woman would win the final victory over Satan, to the benefit of all mankind. In making this first promise of salvation, the Creator of mankind showed that he is also the Saviour of mankind.

THE CALL OF ABRAHAM

The call of Abraham was the starting-point of God's plan to fulfil his promise of salvation. Abraham worshipped idols, as did all his people. But then God revealed himself to Abraham and called him to leave his home in Ur of the Chaldeans. In Genesis 12:1–3 we read how God promises to give Abraham a son, a people and a homeland, and assures him that all the nations of the earth will be blessed through him.

Abraham believes God's promise and demonstrates his faith by obeying God's call. So his faith is credited to him as righteousness.[2] Again God takes the initiative and makes an agreement with Abraham in which God renews his earlier promise.[3] The land of Canaan is promised to Abraham's descendants.[4] However, Abraham himself lived there as an alien in a foreign land,[5] for 'he was looking forward to the city with foundations, whose architect and builder is God'.[6]

The patriarch will be the father not only of a people but also of 'many nations' composed of believers from all over the world.[7] So, then, the promises made to Abraham refer to a specific people and a specific land. But these specific elements are pointers to a much greater whole, involving all the peoples of the world who, because of Abraham's faith, are called to receive an inheritance far greater than the land of Canaan: nothing less than God's righteousness through faith in Jesus Christ.[8]

THE CHOICE OF ISRAEL

Abraham's children, the descendants of his son Isaac, were slaves of the Egyptians for several centuries. Their liberation, under the leadership of Moses, confirms God's plan of redemption. Again, God makes a covenant with the people of Israel by which they become God's chosen people, heirs of the promise made to Abraham and, consequently, inheritors of the land of Canaan.[9]

By choosing Israel, and so fulfilling his promise to Abraham, God shows his sovereign grace: he chooses whoever he wishes in order to reveal himself to mankind. He did not choose Israel because they *deserved* to be chosen; he chose them because he keeps his promises and because of his undeserved love for them.[10] So God's choice is not a sign of favouritism towards the chosen people, nor does it make them in any way superior to other people. The nation of Israel is told to love the foreigners who live in the land and to remember that they, the Israelites, had been foreigners in Egypt, for God cares for the foreigner, and shows no partiality.[11] On the other hand, the people who have been chosen by God are answerable to him. If God's people do not keep to the terms of the agreement, they will have to bear the consequences, including exile in foreign lands.[12]

God's gift of the land of Canaan to Israel was also his free choice: the whole earth belongs to him.[13] The dispossession of the inhabitants of the Promised Land was to be God's punishment for their extreme wickedness.[14]

THE PROMISE FULFILLED

From David . . .
Forsaken by God because he disobeyed God's commands, Saul, the first king of Israel, was replaced as head of God's

people by David. David distinguished himself by the many wars in which he eventually defeated his enemies, made Jerusalem the capital of his kingdom and won control of the whole land of Canaan. When David announced his intention to build a temple for God, his court prophet told him that although his desire was praiseworthy, it would not be fulfilled because, in the prophet's words, 'You are a warrior and have shed blood.'[15] Instead, it was David's son Solomon who was given the task of building the temple. When it was finished there was a great opening ceremony at which Solomon reminded the people how God had kept the promise he made to Moses. The people of Israel were now settled in the Promised Land, just as God had promised.[16] So a part of God's promise to Abraham was fulfilled in the history of Israel.

When Solomon died, the kingdom of Israel was divided into two parts: Israel (known as the northern kingdom) with its capital eventually in Samaria, and Judah (known as the southern kingdom) centred on the city of Jerusalem. From the time of this division there were very few kings who had a respect for God in their hearts. Israel, like its kings, seemed unwilling to return to God's Law.[17] So the prophets were constantly having to condemn the evil actions of the people[18] and to forewarn them of the exile which they would eventually have to suffer.[19] But, along with the prophecy of judgment, there was also the promise of an eventual return to the land[20] and prophecy about the day when God's people would include people from every nation on earth.[21] It was foretold that the future glory of Jerusalem would be far greater than its earlier glory. New prospects were opened for the future of God's chosen people.[22]

In the year 732 BCE (before the Christian era), the kingdom of Israel was invaded by the Assyrians, who carried off its inhabitants and left foreigners to settle in the land. In the year 586 the kingdom of Judah, in its turn, was destroyed by the Babylonians, who sent a large part of the population into exile in Babylon.

In the year 539, however, Cyrus conquered Babylon, and the following year the Jews returned from exile. They started to rebuild the temple and the outer walls of Jerusalem. But the great days of the kings of Israel were gone for ever. It was the end of an era of history, and no prophetic voice was heard for 400 years.

. . . to Jesus Christ

There were very few Jews still patiently waiting for the complete fulfilment of God's promise to Abraham by the time the birth of Jesus was announced to his mother, Mary. But she herself saw this event as the fulfilment of that promise.[23] And Zechariah saw the birth of *his* son, John, as the first sign of the coming of the messianic age.[24] Simeon in the temple, was told by the Holy Spirit that the child he was holding in his arms would one day bring salvation, not just to Israel but to the whole world.[25]

Jesus gathered around him twelve men whom he sent out 'to the lost sheep of Israel'.[26] He later told them, in stirring language, that they would be the twelve judges of the kingdom of God.[27] This kingdom, rejected by Israel, would be given to a new people, made up of Jews and non-Jews,[28] who would take over from the people of Israel.[29] This new age would begin very soon. Because the people of Jerusalem had not recognized the time of God's coming to them,[30] the city of Jerusalem would be taken from the people of Israel and would be 'trampled on by the Gentiles'.[31] The destruction of Jerusalem (which in fact occurred in the year 70 CE) would mark the end of Israel's role in God's plan of salvation and would be a sign of the coming judgment at the end of the age.[32]

Right up to the time of Jesus' ascension his disciples were concerned about the destiny of Israel as a nation. So Jesus, for the last time before he ascended to heaven, had to turn their eyes towards the future of the kingdom of God, which it would be their mission to extend to all the nations of the earth.[33] Only after Pentecost did Jesus' disciples understand that the new people of God would be made up of Jews and Gentiles.[34] The apostle Paul, who also became convinced of this,[35] described the church as 'the Israel of God',[36] the 'Jerusalem that is above',[37] and 'Abraham's seed'.[38] Paul saw the church as inheriting what was once Israel's privilege by natural descent.[39] For Peter, too, the church was the new Israel which had been promised an inheritance that could never perish, an inheritance kept in heaven.[40] The author of the letter to the Hebrews invited the Jewish Christians to whom he wrote to enter into 'God's rest', of which the Promised Land was only a symbol.[41] He told them that the new covenant, founded on better promises, had completely replaced the old covenant.[42] The apostle John, contrasting the church with the synagogue,[43] likens the church to 'the Holy City, the new Jerusalem', which he describes in Revelation chapters 21 and 22 in the kind of language used by the prophets of Israel, notably the post-exilic prophet Zechariah.[44] In fact, the whole unanimous testimony of the apostles can be summed up by quoting just one short statement of faith from the writings of Paul:

'No matter how many promises God had made, they are "Yes" in Christ. And so through him the "Amen" is spoken by us to the glory of God.'[45]

NOT ZIONISM, NOR ANTI-SEMITISM

Even from this brief survey, we can see that the Zionist interpretation of the promise made to Abraham cannot be reconciled with the interpretation of the Old Testament by the New Testament writers who were all, except Luke, 100 per cent Jewish.

This does not mean that the gospel is of no help in solving the Middle-East conflict. A positive approach to this conflict can be derived from the general teaching of Jesus and his apostles. In conclusion, it is worth drawing attention to two important elements of this teaching.

First, the Christian citizens of any state are just as much members of that state as any other of its citizens. Their citizenship of the kingdom of God[46] does not cancel out their duties to the state.[47] They should therefore take a full part in the life of their nation, including its political life, taking into consideration the interests of their fellow-citizens. But, however involved in national affairs they become, Christians must not forget that the New Testament makes a distinction between the kingdom of God on the one hand and the state on the other hand. States which call themselves 'Christian' ignore this distinction just as much as the State of Israel or the Islamic Republics do.

Second, the involvement of Christians in national affairs will be all the more 'prophetic', or significant, if it is guided and enlightened by a knowledge of what the kingdom of God is like, and if Christians are uncompromising in their obedience to the demands of God's kingdom. This kingdom is one of justice and mercy, of truth and peace.[48] Justice *without* mercy is no justice at all in a world where no one can claim to be completely just and fair. Nor will peace last long unless it is accompanied by a spirit of forgiving and forgetting. 'Peace with justice' can therefore never be achieved without love of one's neighbour, even if this neighbour happens to be our enemy.[49]

Real peace must involve deep reconciliation. It cannot be achieved by a crushing defeat of our enemy. The first step towards peace is to achieve a victory over ourselves and over our own feelings of animosity, which are the real obstacles to the solution of any conflict.

Because Zionism is a secular form of the messianic hope, Zionism and Christianity are diametrically opposed. Anti-Semitism (in the strictest sense) is one of the many forms of *not* loving your neighbour, and it is therefore deeply incompatible with Christian faith. And because anti-Zionism sometimes leads to anti-Semitism, many people today confuse the two things. Others deliberately foster this confusion, so deepening the division between Jews and Arabs. This certainly does not help the cause of peace. Peace will not be achieved unless both Zionism and anti-Semitism are called into question.

NOTES

1 For a more detailed study of this subject, see Colin Chapman, *Whose Promised Land?* (Lion Publishing, 1983) and Elias Chacour, *Blood Brothers* (Chosen Books/Zondervan, USA, 1984).
2 OT Genesis 15:6.
3 OT Genesis 17.
4 OT Genesis 17:7–8.
5 OT Genesis 23:4.
6 NT Hebrews 11:9–10.
7 OT Genesis 17:5–6; NT Hebrews 11:12.
8 NT Romans 4:13–25.
9 OT Exodus 6:2–8; 19:4–6.
10 OT Deuteronomy 7:7–8.
11 OT Leviticus 19:33–34; Deuteronomy 10:14–19.
12 OT Deuteronomy 28:62–68.
13 OT Exodus 19:5; Leviticus 25:23.
14 OT Genesis 15:16; Deuteronomy 18:9–12.
15 OT 1 Chronicles 28:3.
16 OT 1 Kings 8:56.
17 OT Isaiah 1:2–3.

18 OT Isaiah 3:1–15.
19 OT Isaiah 5:25–30.
20 OT Jeremiah 25:8–13.
21 OT Isaiah 56:3–8.
22 OT Isaiah 62, 65; Ezekiel 47:22–23.
23 NT Luke 1:54–55.
24 NT Luke 1:68–73.
25 NT Luke 2:29–32.
26 NT Matthew 10:6.
27 NT Matthew 19:28.
28 NT John 10:16.
29 NT Matthew 8:11–12; 21:43.
30 NT Luke 19:41–44.
31 NT Luke 21:24.
32 NT Luke 21:25–36.
33 NT Acts 1:6–8.
34 NT Acts 2:39; 11:18; 15:14–18.
35 NT Acts 13:44–47.
36 NT Galatians 6:16.
37 NT Galatians 4:21–26.
38 NT Galatians 3:28–29.
39 NT Romans 2:25–29; 9:6–8; 9:24–29; 1 Corinthians 10:18.
40 NT 1 Peter 1:4; 2:9–10.
41 NT Hebrews 4.
42 NT Hebrews 8:6–13.
43 NT Revelation 2:9; 3:9.
44 NT Revelation 21–22.
45 NT 2 Corinthans 1:20.
46 NT Philippians 3:20.
47 NT Romans 13:1–7; 1 Peter 2:13–17.
48 NT Matthew 5:6–9.
49 NT Matthew 5:43–48.

3

THE SCRIPTURES: HAVE THEY BEEN FALSIFIED?

Those involved in the dialogue between Muslims and Christians know that sooner or later one question is bound to arise: the question of the authenticity of the Judaeo-Christian Scriptures. It is the source of many of the arguments between Christians and Muslims. It is not always the first question to be raised but, in the last analysis, that is what most of the arguments boil down to. The reason for this is that both faiths are based on revealed Books: the Qur'an and the Bible. So let's begin at the beginning . . .[1]

THE RELATIONSHIP OF THE QUR'AN TO THE BIBLE

The Qur'an teaches that God's word which has been revealed to mankind at various times comes from a heavenly original called 'the Mother of the Book'.[2] There are four separate collections of such revelations in book form:

1. The Torah, revealed through Moses,[3] which is 'a light and a guidance for mankind'.[4]
2. The Zabûr, revealed through David.[5]
3. The gospel, revealed through Jesus, in which there is also guidance and light, and which confirms the

Torah.[6] Jesus followed on from Abraham[7] in preparing the way for Muhammad.[8]

4. The Qur'an, revealed through Muhammad, which is 'a guidance and a blessing,'[9] confirms the Torah and the gospel[10] and explains it.[11] But its authority is greater than the gospel.[12] That is why Muslims are instructed to believe the first three revelations[13] which had prophesied Muhammed's mission.[14]

The 'People of the Book'[15] (i.e. Jews and Christians), who had been called to receive the final revelation (i.e. the Qur'an),[16] did not recognize the divine origin of the Qur'an. Yet the Qur'an still urges Muslims to have faith in the Jewish and Christian Scriptures[17] and it urges the 'People of the Book' to obey those Scriptures.[18]

THE CORRUPTION OF THE SCRIPTURES

What the Qur'an says

About twenty verses in the Qur'an challenge the attitude of Jews and Christians towards their Scriptures. All these verses date from the Medina period and reflect the conflicts between Jews and Muslims in that city. Apart from two verses which specifically refer to the Christians by name,[19] it is the Jews who are blamed for corrupting the revealed truth. They cover up the Muslim character of Abraham's faith in God,[20] and they refuse to pray in the direction of Mecca.[21] They mis-read the Torah[22] and its instructions[23] and they conceal the texts of the Torah,[24] substituting a different book[25] which they read aloud in the same way as the Holy Scriptures, so as to deceive the listeners.[26]

Eight verbs describe the deceitfulness of the 'People of the Book'. The strongest term used is without doubt the verb '*ḥarrafa*' which occurs four times.[27] This verb may be translated 'to falsify'. In Islamic thinking this verb is used to mean the manipulation of the Scriptures and the result of that manipulation. The harsh tone of this Muslim criticism of Jews and Christians goes beyond the tensions which have existed between the Muslims and the other groups down through the centuries: as we shall see later, it is the result of a Muslim concept of revelation being applied to the Scriptures.

What the first Muslim community said

In the documents which tell us about the life of the first Muslim community, we are struck by how little is said about 'falsification'. That in itself suggests that the first-generation Muslims hardly questioned the authority of the Scriptures.

Tabarî (224/839-310/923),[28] the well-known chronicler and commentator on the Qur'an, reports a question put to Muhammad by a Jew who wanted to know whether Muhammad believed that the Torah was God's truth. Muhammad replied that he did, but he added that the Jews had suppressed the teaching of the Torah, broken its covenant and altered its contents.[29]

The opinion of 'Umar, the second caliph, on this matter has been preserved for us in a letter quoted by Dârimî (181/797-255/870), a collector of Islamic traditions. His view is that the monks and the teachers, afraid of losing their position of authority in the eyes of their flock, either distorted the teaching of the Scriptures by false interpretations or else covered up scriptural teaching that was too clear to be misinterpreted.[30]

Ibn 'Abbâs, one of Muhammad's famous companions, was surprised to find Muslims consulting the 'People of the Book' as if the Qur'an had not been revealed. After all, the Word of God in the Qur'an had not been altered by the Muslims, whereas the 'People of the Book' had altered their own Scriptures.[31]

These three accounts, the only ones we have on this

subject, show therefore that the first Muslims accepted the Scriptures as true but condemned the actions of the 'People of the Book'.

What Muslim thinkers have said

There are two main ways of interpreting the Qur'anic verses we are dealing with, and Muslim thinkers are divided into two groups according to which view they hold.

The first group considers that Jews and Christians have misinterpreted their Scriptures but that the text of these Scriptures, or at least most of it, is authentic.

Râzî (543/1149-606/1209), the great commentator on the Qur'an, supports the view that only the Jews have actually altered scriptural teachings, and he throws light on a number of other points. He states that the teachings which have been altered concern either the Torah's references to Muhammad, or the use of whipping instead of stoning as the punishment for adultery, or else those sayings of Muhammad reported by the Jews. The alteration consists either of deliberately leaving words out of the Torah or else of deliberately misinterpreting certain passages. Râzî prefers the misinterpretation theory because, as he points out, the Scriptures were handed down by many witnesses whose versions of the texts agree together (*tawâtur*), and so it is not possible for the text of the Scriptures to have been altered.[32]

Bâqillânî (who died in 403/1013), one of the great theologians, connects the alteration of the Torah by the Jews with the disappearance of the monarchy in Israel. He believes that the alteration was partly the result of errors in interpreting the sacred text, in copying it out and in translating it from one language to another. When he discusses the doctrine of Christ's divinity, he refutes it by giving a rationalistic interpretation of certain verses in the Gospels. But never for a moment does he cast doubt on the Gospels' authority.[33]

Ġazâlî (450/1057-505/1111), another well-known Muslim thinker and mystic, adopts a broadly similar approach. His *Excellent refutation of the divinity of Jesus based on the Gospels* sets out to prove that Christians have misinterpreted the Gospel passages which appear to show Jesus as God. The fact that he bases his arguments on the texts of Scripture shows (unless we dismiss it as purely tactical) that he accepts the authority of those Scriptures.[34]

Muhammad 'Abduh (1265/1849-1323/1905), the great nineteenth-century reformer, in his well-known commentary on the Qur'an, blames only the Jews for the alteration of Scripture. He takes the view that, just as they altered the Torah to reject Jesus Christ, so they misinterpreted passages of the Torah which, in fact, foretell the coming of Muhammad. Like Râzî, he likens this Jewish misinterpretation of the Scriptures to certain Muslim extremists' misinterpretation of the Qur'an. He then states quite openly that he believes the text of the Gospels to be authentic.[35]

The second group of thinkers, less representative of traditional Islamic thought, takes the view that the 'People of the Book' have falsified the text of Scripture itself.

Ġuwaynî (who died in 478/1085) is the author of a polemical treatise on the falsification of the Scriptures. He begins his argument by offering a proof of this falsification. According to Ġuwaynî, Jews and Christians deny that the coming of Muhammad was foretold in their Scriptures, but the Qur'an clearly states that it *was* foretold. The present-day Jewish Torah, which contradicts the Greek version used by Christians, was composed by Ezra in the sixth century BCE. The Gospels, which differ in their accounts of the same events, were compiled many years after the events, which explains the differences.[36]

Ibn Ḥazm (384/994-456/1064), the writer of a book which deals with the history of religions, lists all the contradictions he finds between the Torah and history, geography, morality, reason itself . . . and, especially, the Qur'an. He accuses the Gospel writers of lying by portraying Jesus as God when in fact Jesus called himself the Son of man. Because he follows a literal interpretation of the Qur'an, Ibn Ḥazm interprets the Scriptures in the same way. This leads him to emphasize textual discrepancies which might have been resolved by someone taking a broader view of the text.[37]

The criticisms levelled at the 'People of the Book' by Muslim writers raise many questions which cannot be discussed in detail here. We must be content with a brief answer to some which often cause confusion.

REVELATION AND SCRIPTURE

What is 'revelation'?
In Islamic thought, 'revelation' basically means a book: the Torah, the Zabûr, the gospel, the Qur'an. Prophets are messengers who pass on this revelation. The Qur'an is the Word of God and Muhammad is the one who conveyed this word to mankind. What is written in the Qur'an is primarily the revelation of God's will which can be understood by human minds.

This is quite different from the way that Christians think of *their* Scriptures. For Christians, the Bible contains God's revelation of himself and it goes beyond what human minds can understand. For Christians, revelation consists of God's actions as well as his words. The words explain the actions, and the actions confirm the truth of the words. In the days of Moses the climax of God's revelation was Israel's deliverance from Egypt and the giving of the Law. So the Torah is the written account of how God revealed himself through the history of the people of

Israel. The Torah is therefore important because of the important events it records.

For Christians, God's revelation reached its climax 2,000 years ago in the person of Jesus Christ, who is God's Word in the form of a real human being made of flesh and blood. So Jesus Christ is himself God's revelation and his apostles are the messengers who pass on this revelation to mankind. The gospel is the good news which Jesus proclaimed in his words and his actions. So his miracles are signs, confirming the truth of his words. This point can be illustrated from the miracles of Jesus which are mentioned in the Qur'an. His healing of the blind is a symbol of the light that he brings to those who, because of their spiritual blindness, have invented their own idea of God. Jesus' healing of the lepers is a sign that he restores mankind to spiritual health. And Jesus' raising of the dead shows he brings back to life those who are spiritually dead.

It follows, from this concept of revelation, that the *spiritual* meaning of the events recorded in the Gospels is more important than (though it does not detract from) their historical truth. A proper reading of the Gospels cannot, therefore, be limited to the literal meaning of the texts and to the historical events alone. A proper reading of the Gospels involves trying to bring out the underlying significance of the reported events. Once you have discovered this deeper level of meaning, you begin to unearth an infinite wealth of understanding from what at first seemed to be all contradiction and confusion.

Given the Judaeo-Christian concept of what revelation is, anyone seeking to understand the Scriptures will not rely too much on their own intelligence because the ultimate interpreter of the Scriptures is the very same God who is revealed in them.

How did revelation come about?
The verb '*anzala*' (or '*nazzala*'), which is used in the

Qur'an to describe how revelation happened, conveys the idea of something being sent or brought down from above. Thus, according to Islamic tradition, Muhammad repeated word for word the revelations given to him by the angel Gabriel.[38] So it is that the book in which all these revelations were written down has the title 'Qur'an', which means literally 'recitation'. Naturally, then, this book is considered as nothing less than the Word of God. By the same token, even the very best translations of the Qur'an cannot be the Word of God because God revealed his Word in Arabic. This is how the Qur'an speaks not only of its own revelation but also of the biblical revelation. However, even if this concept of revelation were true of the Qur'an, it is not really true of the Bible.

In the case of the Bible, revelation did not come through the angel Gabriel but through the Holy Spirit who inspired the Scriptures. The Holy Spirit was responsible for their composition while at the same time allowing for the human characteristics both of the writers and of their intended readers. He made full use of the individual abilities of the Gospel writers and of their religious and cultural background. The ways in which the Holy Spirit inspired them varied according to their individual personalities and allowed for their individual liberty.

The fact that the Scriptures are inspired means that they can properly be called the Word of God as well as the words of men. Furthermore, good translations of the Scriptures may be regarded as the equivalent of the original texts and thus as God's Word. This means that the reader can study the Scriptures in the same way he studies other books. He can make use of all the available resources of human knowledge — knowledge of languages and literature in particular — which may help him to examine the texts of Scripture more thoroughly and to understand them better. He will certainly try to look at the text from all possible angles without trying to force any one interpretation onto it. He will take into account what kind of text it is (whether it is historical, poetic, prophetic, narrative, apocalyptic or wisdom literature), and he will thus decide how he should go about interpreting it.

In short, if we accept this Christian understanding of revelation, we cannot approach the Scriptures with the literalism of an Ibn Ḥazm or a Ǧuwaynî, nor with the rationalism of a Bâqillânî or a Ġazâlî. What we need instead is a thorough and open-minded study of the Scriptures, enlightened by the Spirit of God who inspired them.

How was the revelation passed on?

According to Islamic tradition, the first attempt to compile the Qur'anic suras was made during the reign of the first caliph, on the orders of 'Umar. This semi-official compilation was entrusted, finally, to Ḥafṣa, the daughter of 'Umar and one of Muhammad's wives. Four other collections of writings were then in circulation at Kûfa, Damascus, Baṣra and Ḥoms. They were still in use when 'Uthmân, the third caliph, (644–656), established the 'definitive' text of the Qur'an. It was based on Ḥafṣa's compilation, which was the most widely accepted version in Medina. 'Uthmân ordered all the other versions to be destroyed. His decision did not please the Shi'a Muslims, who believed that their teachings were more clearly supported by the Kûfa collection than by 'Uthmân's.[39]

The original text of the official version has not survived, and our earliest fragments of the Qur'an date from the second century. This text is the only one on whose manuscripts our editions of the Qur'an are based, yet it contains a number of variant readings. In the year 322/923 the number of such readings was officially limited to seven, because of a statement attributed to Muhammad, though this limit was subsequently raised to ten and then to fourteen.[40]

The Gospels, based on earlier source material, were

written during the second half of the first century CE, and Christian writings from the first half of the second century quote freely from them. From the beginning of the second half of the second century the authority of the Gospels, which was becoming more and more accepted by Christians, superseded the authority given to other similar writings, yet these other writings were not banned. From the end of the second century the Gospels were accepted as part of the canon of Scripture.

We no longer possess the original manuscripts of the Gospels. The oldest fragments which have come down to us date from the middle of the second century CE. The thousands of ancient manuscripts of the Gospels, complete or partial, and the fairly recent discovery of the Dead Sea Scrolls, have enabled textual critics to establish that the text of the Scriptures, despite its many minor variant readings, has come down to us remarkably well preserved. The same can hardly be said of the Qur'an because of the relatively small number of its manuscripts and because these are all copies from just one original.

This brief survey of the history of the biblical and Qur'anic texts shows that the text of the Bible is at least as reliable as that of the Qur'an. From a purely historical viewpoint, it seems difficult to claim that the biblical texts have been falsified. Any such claim could only be based on *a priori* arguments which do not square with the facts.

The Gospel of Barnabas

Well-meaning Muslims sometimes claim that the only authentic Gospel is the Gospel of Barnabas, which contains the real teaching of Jesus. But what are the facts of the case?

Firstly, we must take note that, according to all the experts who have studied it, this document, which is in Italian, can be no older than the sixteenth century CE. It therefore has nothing to do with the Epistle of Barnabas which dates from the second century. Its alleged author,

Barnabas, was the man appointed to replace Thomas in the group of the twelve apostles. In fact the real author was an Italian converted to Islam. In this Gospel, Jesus denies that he is the Son of God and even sends his disciples to correct those who had taken him to be God. He himself is not the Messiah, but he announces the coming of the Messiah whose name will be Muhammad and who will be descended from Abraham via his son Ishmael. In this Gospel Jesus is not crucified, but Judas, his betrayer, is mistaken for him and crucified in his place. Jesus' disciples come during the night, steal the body (of Judas) and claim that Jesus has risen from the dead. In fact, according to this Gospel, he had been carried up by three angels into the third heaven before he could be arrested. Then he comes back for a short while, escorted by these same angels, to comfort Mary and his disciples. He is now in heaven and will return to the earth before the end of time to correct what Christians have taught about him, to die and be raised at the last day.

This picture of Jesus is so close to the traditional Islamic teaching about him that it leaves us in no doubt as to the author's apologetic intent. He makes the mistake, however, of having Jesus say that he is not the Messiah, contrary to the teaching of the Qur'an. Nor does he seem to know much about the geography of Palestine, as he places the town of Nazareth on the shores of Lake Galilee. Since both distance and time separate this writer from Jesus, his apocryphal writing can hardly give us a true account of Jesus' life.[41]

DID THE SCRIPTURES FORETELL THE COMING OF MUHAMMAD?

The Qur'an asserts that the Scriptures had predicted the coming of Muhammad, but it makes no reference to any particular scriptural text to back up this assertion. Buḫârî tells us that when one of Muhammad's companions asked how the Torah described Muhammad, he replied:

'The Torah describes him in the same terms as the Qur'an: "O Prophet, we have sent you as a witness, to preach, warn and defend the ignorant. You are my servant and my apostle; I have called you the One Who Trusts (in God). [This prophet] is neither harsh nor hard-hearted nor does he shout his message in the market-places. He does not return evil for evil: he is kind-hearted and forgiving. God will not call him to be with himself until he has set the lost people back on the right path. Then they will say: 'there is no god but God'. Thus he will open the eyes of the blind, the ears of the deaf and the hardened hearts." '[42]

These words are distant echoes of the Bible's first Servant Song.[43] A careful reading of this text is bound to bring out the contrast between the Servant's peaceful mission and Muhammad's mission, which was marked by a series of wars. The Gospel writer Matthew, commenting on Jesus' command to those he had healed not to spread the news of his miracles, quotes the above-mentioned prophecy of Isaiah which he believes to have been fulfilled in Jesus.[44] The other Servant Songs, particularly the fourth which describes the Servant's sufferings with incomparable beauty,[45] are sufficient proof, if such were needed, that these prophecies can refer only to Jesus.

Muhammad 'Abduh refers not only to Isaiah but also to the Pentateuch.[46] The author may be thinking of the prophecy about 'the new Moses'.[47] It is clear from this passage that the new Moses will be descended from the people of Israel, which is clearly not true of the Arab prophet.

The author of a recent book claims that Muhammad is

the 'paraclete' whose coming was foretold by Jesus.[48] But chapters 14 to 16 of John's Gospel and chapter 1 of the Book of Acts leave us in no doubt that the promised 'paraclete' is none other than the Holy Spirit,[49] the Spirit of Truth[50] which the disciples would receive, during their lifetime, in Jerusalem.

To sum up, then, the theory that the Bible has been falsified seems to have originated largely because the Qur'anic concept of revelation was applied to the Scriptures. It shows a misunderstanding of the biblical concept of revelation and of the theological principles and historical facts which follow from it. Muslim intellectuals today are better informed as to what revelation means to the Christian and they are much more ready to accept the authenticity of the Scriptures than their predecessors. It was earlier generations of Muslim thinkers who made an article of faith out of a few Qur'anic critical references to the attitude of the 'People of the Book' towards their own Scriptures.

NOTES

1 This chapter is the summary of a DEA (*Diplôme d'Etudes Approfondies*) paper, presented by the author at the University of Paris, on 'The alteration of the Judaeo-Christian Scriptures according to the Qur'an and Islamic tradition' (November 1982).

2 Q sura 13 (Al-Ra'd):39; sura 43 (Al-Zukhruf):4.

3 Q sura 3 (Al-'Imrân):93; sura 6 (Al-An'âm):154.

4 Q sura 6 (Al-An'âm):91.

5 Q sura 4 (Al-Nisâ'):163; sura 17 (Al-Isrâ'):55; sura 21 (Al-Anbiyâ'):105.

6 Q sura 5 (Al-Mâ'ida):46.
7 Q sura 2 (Al-Baqara):129.
8 Q sura 61 (Al-Ṣaff):6.
9 Q sura 6 (Al-An'âm):157.
10 Q sura 2 (Al-Baqara):91; sura 3 (Al-'Imrân):3, 81; sura 4 (Al-Nisâ'):47.
11 Q sura 6 (Al-An'âm):114; sura 10 (Yûnis):37; sura 12 (Yûsuf):111.
12 Q sura 5 (Al-Mâ'ida):48.
13 Q sura 3 (Al-'Imrân):84; sura 4 (Al-Nisâ'):136; sura 5 (Al-Mâ'ida):59.
14 Q sura 7 (Al-A'râf):157.
15 The words 'People of the Book' translate the Qur'anic expression '*Ahl al-Kitâb*' ('those to whom the Scriptures have been entrusted') which is used to refer to Jews and Christians.
16 Q sura 2 (Al-Baqara):41; sura 4 (Al-Nisâ'):47.
17 Q sura 3 (Al-'Imrân):119; sura 4 (Al-Nisâ'): 136.
18 Q sura 5 (Al-Mâ'ida):66, 68.
19 Q sura 2 (Al-Baqara):140; sura 5 (Al-Mâ'ida):14.
20 Q sura 2 (Al-Baqara):140.
21 Q sura 2 (Al-Baqara):146.
22 Q sura 4 (Al-Nisâ'):46.
23 Q sura 5 (Al-Mâ'ida):41.
24 Q sura 6 (Al-An'âm):91.
25 Q sura 2 (Al-Baqara):79.
26 Q sura 2 (Al-'Imrân):78.
27 Q sura 2 (Al-Baqara):75; sura 4 (Al-Nisâ'):46; sura 5 (Al-Mâ'ida):13, 41.
28 The first number in brackets refers to the Islamic Era based on the year of Hijrah (622 CE).
29 See Ṭabarî, *al-Tafsîr* (Cairo: Ḥalabî, 1388/1968), on Qur'an, sura 5 (Al-Mâ'ida):68.
30 See Dârimî, *Sunan* (Medina, 1386/1966), 'Muqaddima' 56.
31 See Buḫârî, *Ṣaḥiḥ* (Cairo, 1378/1958), 'Šahâdât' 29.
32 See Râzî, *al-Tafsîr al-Kabîr* (Cairo, 1352/1933) on Qur'an, sura 4 (Al-Nisâ'):46; sura 5 (Al-Mâ'ida):13, 41; sura 2 (Al-Baqara):75.
33 Bâqillânî, *Kitâb-al-Tamhîd* (Beirut, Librairie Orientale,

1957), chapters 8 and 13.

34   Ġazâlî *al-Radd al-ğamîl li-ilâhiyyat 'Îsâ bi-ṣarîḥ al Inğîl*.
     Text edited and translated, with commentary, by R.
     Chidiac: *Refutation excellente de la divinité de Jésus-Christ
     d'après les évangiles* [*Excellent Refutation of the Divinity of
     Jesus Based on the Gospels*], Paris: Presses Universitaires
     de France, 1939.

35   Muhammad 'Abduh, *Tafsîr al-Manâr* (Cairo, Dar al-
     Manâr), on Qur'an, sura 2: 159 and 185, and sura 3:78.

36   Ġuwaynî *Šifa' al-ġalîl fi bayân mâ waqa 'a fi-l-Tawrât
     wa-l-Inğîl min-al-Tabdîl*. Text edited by M. Allard, *Textes
     apologétiques de Ġuwaynî* (Beirut, Dâr al-Masriq, 1968).

37   Ibn Ḥazm *Kitâb al-fiṣal fi-l-milal wa-l-ahwa' wa-l-niḥal*
     (Cairo, 1320/1902, reprinted 1400/1980).

38   See Buḥârî *Ṣaḥiḥ* 'Bad' al-waḥy', 2 and 3.

39   See A. Jeffrey, *Materials for the history of the text of the
     Qur'an* (Leiden: E. J. Brill, 1937).

40   Buḥârî, *Ṣaḥiḥ* 'Ḥuṣûmât', 4.

41   See L. Cirillo and M. Frenaux *Evangile de Barnabé* [*The
     Gospel of Barnabas*]. Research into its composition and
     origin, text and translation (Paris, 1977). J. Slomp, 'The
     gospel in dispute', *Islamochristiania* (Rome, 1978); J. Jomier,
     A persistent enigma: the so-called Gospel of Barnabas
     (Beirut, 1980).

42   Buḥârî *Ṣaḥiḥ* 'Buyû'', 50.

43   OT Isaiah 42:1–4.

44   NT Matthew 12:15–21.

45   OT Isaiah 52:13 – 53:12.

46   See Muhammad 'Abduh, *Tafsîr al-Manâr* on Qur'an sura
     2:159.

47   OT Deuteronomy 18:15–19.

48   M. Bucaille, *La Bible, le Coran et la Science* [*The Bible, the
     Qur'an and Science*] (Paris, 1978).

49   NT John 14:26.

50   NT John 14:17; 15:26; 16:13.

4

MAN: THE FRIEND OF GOD?

Our definition of mankind's relationship to God will depend, of course, on our definition of God, and, consequently, of mankind. So, before we can answer this question, we need to look at the concept of God as found in Islam and Christianity.

WHO IS GOD?

In Islam, God is the One Being; he is the Creator, he is eternal, personal, sovereign, powerful, holy, just, wise and transcendent. When the Muslim says God is 'transcendent', he means that he is radically other than, and totally separate from, his creation, including mankind.[1] That does not imply that he is distant from mankind. The Qur'an affirms that God is closer to man than his own jugular vein.[2] God communicates with man, sends him prophets and apostles, reveals the Law to him, and shows him his will. But the reality of God, i.e. who God really is, remains inaccessible to us. His names and his attributes certainly give us some idea of who and what he is, and the ninety-nine most beautiful names of God which Muslim theology recognizes[3] unveil God's person to some extent. But the hundredth and most high name[4] remains unknown, unless it is the actual name of God, 'Allah'. God loves those who obey his will[5] but not those who disobey.[6] He accepts people's repentance,[7] for he is a relenting God.[8] He forgives men their faults, for he is merciful; all the Qur'anic suras, except the ninth, begin with the invocation: 'In the name of Allah, the Compassionate, the Merciful'. His mercy is but one of God's innumerable favours.[9] But this mercy only serves to reveal more clearly God's majesty as judge of all his creatures. He, indeed, is the fairest of judges.[10] His love is shown to mankind by the gift of his Law, the forgiveness of sins, the blessings he showers on mankind and his rewards for people's good actions. In all these things God remains absolutely transcendent: his transcendence would be threatened if his love came into personal contact with human beings.

These characteristics of God are very similar to those we find in the Bible, but the Bible gives other characteristics in addition to those we have seen in the Qur'an, which are no less important. The God of the Torah does not simply communicate words: he reveals himself to mankind. In the Sinai covenant, often referred to in the Qur'an, God makes himself party to an agreement with his people. He is, of course, the Creator — but he is also the Redeemer. He is the one who frees Israel from their slavery in Egypt and who reveals to Moses his own name, YHWH.[11] God loves all men equally, even those who disobey him, for his love is unconditional.[12] He also commands his people to love the alien, just as he does.[13] In Jesus Christ God gives himself to mankind, makes a covenant with us, forgives our sins and so teaches us that although he is our judge — and he certainly *is* — he is first and foremost our Father.[14] The glorious God demonstrated his glory in loving us so much that in Jesus Christ he gave himself for our salvation. For God is love.[15]

Muslims generally consider it degrading for God to be a Father. The word carries with it the idea of a mother, sons and daughters.[16] In the end this puts God's creatures on the same level as their Creator who 'begot none, nor was begotten'.[17] Islam's central belief is, after all, not only God's existence but his oneness.

When Christians call God their Father, they do so in two senses. Firstly, in the sense that God is the Creator. Christians believe that men are unique creatures, unlike any others. They believe that the relationship God wanted to establish with mankind is, consequently, a privileged relationship. This in no way implies that mankind in any sense shares God's nature. Even less does it imply that mankind has a mother who took part in God's creative act.

Secondly, in the sense that God is the Redeemer. By calling God 'Father', Christians bear witness to the fact that God the Saviour, as revealed in Jesus Christ, has given them the immense privilege of being adopted as his sons and daughters. This shows what an intimate relationship they have with God, but in no way does it imply that they have become divine beings. They have become sons and daughters of God, not by natural birth, but by adoption.

Bowing before God's unfathomable and transcendent nature, Muslims say *what* God is. Receiving his love, which is all the more unfathomable because it has been given to us to experience, Christians confess *who* God is.[18]

IS MAN THE IMAGE OF GOD?

According to the Qur'an, man is God's supreme creation and his steward on earth.[19] The Muslim is also God's servant and his role is to glorify God by obeying his Law. His submission to God is seen both in his faith in God, his angels, his books, his apostles, the Last Judgment and predestination, and also in his observance of the Five Pillars of Islam — the confession of faith, prayer, almsgiving, fasting and pilgrimage. The Muslim's love for God, referred to several times in the Qur'an,[20] is generally

understood to mean love of his word or of his commandments and only rarely as love of his person. The etymological
meaning of the word 'islam' perfectly illustrates the
essential nature of man's relationship to God. It means the
trusting 'submission' of the servant to his divine master,
not out of fear or forced obedience as unbelieving Muslims
do[21] but out of love for his will. This is the call to all people
proclaimed loud and clear by the Qur'an.

A saying attributed to Muhammad declares that God
created Adam in his own image. Muslim writers are
divided into three main groups in their interpretation of
this saying.

- The first group, not typical of Muslim thought, draws
  the conclusion that God is a body and that man was
  made in the likeness of this body.[22]
- The second group concludes that God made Adam, the
  first man, in his image, and so all men resemble their
  original ancestor.
- The third group explains God's image in man in terms of
  man's stewardship. Consequently, man possesses certain
  divine attributes such as life, knowledge, perfection,
  will and speech.[23]

In the book of Genesis God says: 'Let us make man in
our image, in our likeness'.[24] Christian thinkers have
drawn from this verse the conclusion that man exists in a
face-to-face relationship with God and therefore can
communicate with him. They also conclude that, in his
relationship to the created world, man stands as God's
representative on earth, and that man, as God's most
privileged creature, shares to some extent some of God's
attributes. In these three ways man can be called 'the
image of God on earth'.

Looked at in this light, human relationships can be seen
as reflections of the relationship between God and man, in
that each human being encounters in his fellow human a
creature made in the image of God. This reflection, or

analogy, is most fully expressed in the special bond between man and woman within marriage. Marital love is the best human illustration of God's love for mankind and man's love for God.[25]

A teacher of the Law once asked Jesus: 'Which is the greatest of all the commandments?' and Jesus answered: ' "Love the Lord your God with all your heart, and with all your soul and with all your mind." This is the first and greatest commandment. And the second is like it: "Love your neighbour as yourself." All the Law and the Prophets hang on these two commandments.'[26]

This commandment is indeed two-edged, because love of God cannot be divorced from love of one's neighbour, who is the image of God.[27] Love therefore does not abolish the Law: it sums it up and perfectly fulfils it. Jesus, the perfect image of the invisible God[28] calls his disciples not 'servants' but 'friends' because, he says, 'a servant does not know his master's business. Instead, I have called you friends, for everything that I learned from my Father I have made known to you.'[29]

Abraham, the father and example to all believers,[30] is called God's intimate friend in the Old Testament,[31] the New Testament[32] and in the Qur'an.[33] Islam reserves this privilege for prophets and saints; the Bible sees *all* believers as called to enter into an intimate relationship with God without this involving any change or intermixing of divine and human natures. This relationship of mankind to God as of children to a father is the remarkable privilege bestowed on man by his gracious Creator.

While considering the definition of man's relationship to God as held by mainstream Islam, we must not ignore the view held by Sufism. This spiritual movement has had a profound effect on many Muslims and its influence is still felt today. It emphasizes inner faith, the importance of love and the union between the believer and God. The relationship between the Sufi and God can be illustrated by

that beautiful saying attributed to Râbi'a al-'adawiyya,
one of Islam's first Sufis:

> O Lord!
> If it is the fear of hell which make me pray to you
> then throw me into hell;
> If it is the desire for paradise
> then let me not enter paradise;
> But if I draw near to you for your own sake
> do not hide from me your eternal beauty.[34]

NOTES

1   Q sura 42 (Al-Shûra):11.
2   Q sura 50 (Qâf):16.
3   Q sura 7 (Al-A'râf):180; sura 17 (Al-Isrâ'):110; sura 20 (Ṭa
    Ha):7; sura 59 (Al-Ḥashr):24.
4   Q sura 87 (Al-A'la):1.
5   Q sura 2 (Al-Baqara):195, 222; sura 3 (Al-'Imrân): 31, 76,
    146, 159; sura 5 (Al-Mâ'ida):42; sura 9 (Al-Tawba):4, 108;
    sura 61 (Al-Ṣaff):4.
6   Q sura 2 (Al-Baqara):190; sura 3 (Al-'Imrân):32, 57; sura 4
    (Al-Nisâ'):36, 107; sura 5 (Al-Mâ'ida):64; sura 7 (Al-
    A'râf):31; sura 16 (Al-Naḥl):23; sura 22 (Al-Ḥajj):38; sura
    28 (Al-Qaṣas):76; sura 31 (Luqmân):18.
7   Q sura 42 (Al-Shûra):25; sura 40 (Ghâfir):3.
8   Q sura 2 (Al-Baqara):37, 54, 128, 160.
9   Q sura 16 (Al-Naḥl):18.
10 Q sura 11 (Hûd):45; sura 95 (Al-Tîn):8.
11 OT Exodus 3:13–15.
12 NT John 3:16.
13 OT Deuteronomy 10:17–18.
14 NT Matthew 6:9–15.
15 NT 1 John 4: 8, 16.

16   Q sura 6 (Al-An'âm):101.
17   Q sura 112 (Al-Ikhlâṣ):3.
18   NT Romans 11:33–36.
19   Q sura 2 (Al-Baqara):30; sura 6 (Al-An'âm):165.
20   Q sura 2 (Al-Baqara):165; sura 3 (Al-'Imrân):31; sura 5 (Al-Mâ'ida):54.
21   Q sura 49 (Al-Ḥujurât):14.
22   Muslims who conceive of God as a body are known as 'al-muğassima': 'the corporalists'.
23   See Nîsâbûrî, *Garâ'ib al-Qur'an wa rağâ'ib al-furqân*, (Cairo, 1381/1962) on Qur'an sura 6:164.
24   OT Genesis 1:26; NT James 3:9.
25   See H. Blocher, *In the Beginning* (IVP, 1984).
26   NT Matthew 22:34–40.
27   NT 1 John 4:20–21.
28   NT Colossians 1:15.
29   NT John 15:15.
30   OT Genesis 17:5; NT Romans 4:9–12; Q sura 60 (Al-Mumtaḥana):4, 6.
31   OT Isaiah 41:8.
32   NT James 2:23.
33   Q sura 4 (Al-Nisâ'):125.
34   Quoted by F. M. Pareja, *Islamologie* (Beirut, Imprimerie Catholique, 1964) chapter XIV, 'la mystique'.

5

JESUS CHRIST: CRUCIFIED?

The theme of Jesus' person, as well as his death and resurrection, takes us to the heart of the debate between Christians and Muslims. It is well known that the major disagreements between the two groups centre on the figure of Jesus and, by extension, on God himself. Before dealing with the question of Jesus' death in this chapter, it would be useful, and indeed necessary, to sum up what the Qur'an teaches about Jesus. This teaching is found in fifteen suras and ninety-three verses of the Qur'an.

JESUS IN THE QUR'AN

In the Qur'an we read that the angels called out to Zacharias, when he was in the Shrine praying to God for descendants.[1] They foretold the unexpected birth of a son who would 'confirm the Word of God . . . be princely and chaste, a prophet and a righteous man'.[2]

The Virgin Mary is also told of the birth of 'a Word from God. His name is the Messiah, Jesus the son of Mary. He shall be noble in this world and in the next, and shall be favoured by God. He shall preach to men in his cradle as in the prime of manhood, and shall lead a righteous life'.[3] From the cradle, indeed, Jesus defended his mother against the accusation of adultery and declared that he himself was a servant of God and a prophet.[4] The miraculous coming of Jesus into the world, thanks to the in-breathing of God's Spirit into his mother's womb,[5] is an act of mercy from God.[6] And so this divine favour bestowed on Jesus and Mary[7] makes Jesus and his mother a sign from God to all men.[8]

God instructed Jesus in the Scriptures and in wisdom, in the Torah and in the gospel.[9] But the message specially entrusted to Jesus is the gospel, the good news[10] which, as a faithful servant of God,[11] he preached as a guide and light on men's pathway.[12] This gospel fills the heart of those who receive it with compassion and mercy.[13]

As an apostle of God sent to the children of Israel,[14] Jesus was set before them as an example.[15] As a man blessed by God,[16] he called them to serve God,[17] thus confirming the Torah but overruling some of its prohibitions.[18] Strengthened by the Holy Spirit,[19] he performed miracles with God's permission, among which were the healing of the blind and lepers, and the raising of the dead.[20]

Despite these 'signs' proving that he was sent by God,[21] Jesus succeeded in gathering around him only a handful of men, the apostles, whom God protected against their enemies.[22] The Israelites as a whole tried to put him to death. But God intervened and foiled their plot, because God is the supreme plotter.[23]

How did God foil the plot? Our answer to this question will determine the answer to the question we asked at the beginning of this chapter.

THE TEXTS

To answer the question we need to look at four texts. The first is what Jesus is reported to have said when he was still in the cradle: 'Peace on me the day I was born, and the day I die, and the day I shall be raised alive!'[24] This blessing which Jesus speaks of is like the blessing God pronounces on John the Baptist: 'Peace on him the day he was born, and the day he died and the day he shall be raised alive.'[25] The verbs which are used in both these verses are the following:

- 'walada': to beget.
- 'mâta': to die. This is the commonest verb denoting death in the Arabic language.
- 'ba'ata': to be raised to life. This is one of the two verbs denoting resurrection in the Qur'an. The other is 'qâma', to rise again.

The use of these verbs, and the repetition of the same blessing for Jesus as for John the Baptist, his forerunner, would seem to suggest that Jesus will die and be raised to life like everyone else, including the prophets. However, other information from the Qur'an throws a different light on the situation.

The second text is the answer given by Jesus, in the Qur'an, to a question God asks him about his preaching:

'Then God will say: "Jesus, son of Mary, did you ever say to mankind: 'Worship me and my mother as gods beside God?' "

' "Glory to You," he will answer, "how could I say that to which I have no right? If I have ever said so, You would have surely known it. You know what is in my mind, but I cannot tell what is in Yours. You alone know what is hidden. I spoke to them of nothing except what You bade me. I said: 'Serve Allah, my Lord and your Lord.' I watched over them whilst living in their midst, and ever since You took me to You, You Yourself have been watching over them. You are the witness of all things." '[26]

The last part of this passage uses the verb 'tawaffa', which literally means 'to receive', 'to take back', or 'to collect' (a debt). It has become the commonest verb in Arabic used to express the action of 'causing someone's death'. This shift in meaning, which has occurred in many other languages, is explained by the fact that people have always tried to lessen the horror of death. Moreover, for believers, and for Muslims in particular, death is seen as the moment when the Creator calls his creature to himself. This meaning of '*tawaffa*', the return to God in death, is well attested by the Qur'an. God calls to himself the souls of people while they sleep, keeps those whose death he has decreed, and sends back the others until the day when he finally calls them to himself.[27]

So, in his reply to God, Jesus refers to his death in completely natural terms.

The third passage comes immediately after the verse which states that God is more cunning than the Jews who have plotted against Jesus. It tells us how God will go about foiling their plot. God says:

'Jesus, I am about to cause you to die and lift you up to Me. I shall take you away from the unbelievers and exalt your followers above them till the Day of Resurrection. Then to Me you shall all return and I shall judge your disputes.'[28]

Here again we have the verb '*tawaffa*', followed by the verb '*rafa'a*' meaning 'to lift up'. The order in which these verbs appear suggests that this 'lifting up' means resurrection from death towards the One who causes men to die and rise again. If that is indeed the meaning of this verse, then God's triumph over the Jews who killed Jesus consists, in fact, of lifting Jesus up to God through his resurrection from the dead.

We find this interpretation echoed in the writings of Ibn 'Abbâs, the father of Qur'anic exegesis, who understands '*tawaffa*' in the sense of 'to cause to die'. Those who hold this interpretation conclude that Jesus was 'lifted up' only a few hours after his death.[29]

It should be noted, at this point, that the interpretation most commonly held by Muslims is quite different. It is based chiefly on the last text which we have yet to examine. This text is part of a long and lively argument directed against the Jews. It reads as follows:

> 'They [the Jews] declared: "We have put to death the Messiah Jesus the son of Mary, the apostle of God." They did not kill him, nor did they crucify him, but they thought they did.
>
>   Those that disagreed about him were in doubt concerning his death, for what they knew about it was sheer conjecture; they were not sure that they had slain him. God lifted him up to His presence; He is mighty and wise. There is none among the "People of the Book" but will believe in him before his death; and on the Day of Resurrection he will be witness against them.'[30]

According to Râzî, one of the great figures of Muslim orthodoxy, this verse clearly shows that Jesus was not killed by the Jews: in fact, they killed someone else who took on his likeness. 'Those that disagreed about him' are either the Christians, who are divided into three groups in their interpretation of Jesus' death (the Nestorians, the Melkites and the Jacobites), or the Jews, who, once they realized what the situation was, no longer felt sure that they had really killed Jesus. Jesus had, in fact, been lifted up to heaven by God.[31]

Most Muslim commentators make a connection between sura 4:159 and sura 43:61 in which Jesus is called 'a sign [for the coming of] the Hour [of Judgment]' (Yousuf Ali translation). They also connect it with sayings attributed to Muhammad — and reported by, among others, Ṭabarî — concerning Jesus' return to earth at the end of time. The conclusion they draw from these connections is that Jesus will return to earth before the Day of Resurrection. He will destroy the false Messiah, and will bring about the triumph of Islam and a world-wide reign of peace. Jews and Christians will then believe in him in the same way that Muslims do today. He will then die and be buried by the Muslims. At the Last Day he will be raised to life like everyone else and he will be a witness against the Jews who rejected him and the Christians who made a god of him.[32]

Those who hold this view interpret sura 3:55 in two different ways. For some, who understand 'tawaffa' in the sense of 'to recall', this verse does not refer to the death of Jesus: his ascension into heaven explains how God 'recalled' him. But this meaning of the verb 'tawaffa' — God calling to himself a person in bodily form — is found nowhere in the Qur'an. For others, the conjunction 'and' does not mean that the one event occurs *after* the other. So these people place Jesus' death at the end of time. But the verse in question does not allow for any events involving Jesus in the period between his ascension and the Day of Resurrection. What this verse *does* promise is that Jesus' disciples will be given victory over their enemies who have not accepted that Jesus is a prophet of God.

The fundamental concept which underlies this interpretation of the verse is quite simply God's justice. God gives victory to those who seek to make his cause victorious.[33] That is how it was with Abraham, Lot, Noah,[34] Moses[35] and, lastly, Muhammad, who overcome his enemies. In other words, if God had allowed such a great prophet as Jesus to be handed over to his executioners and so put to death, God's justice would have been denied and Jesus' message discredited. Consequently he had to rescue Jesus and save him from the unjust, shameful and cruel death to which the Jews had condemned him.

This interpretation has the advantage of being supported

by the overwhelming majority of Muslim tradition. According to L. Massignon, the interpretation began to appear in Sunni commentaries in the second half of the second Islamic century, after certain Shiʻa extremists' teachings had been applied retrospectively to Jesus. These Shiʻa made gods of their imams and claimed that, whenever one of these imams met with a violent death, it had happened to someone else who looked just like him, so that the imams should appear to have suffered the tragic fate to which their enemies had subjected them.[36]

The official Islamic interpretation, then, seems to do justice to the meaning of sura 4:157–59. Its main weaknesses are that it is hard to reconcile with the *obvious* meaning of sura 3:55, and that it dates from a later period and has dubious origins. But is it actually possible to understand sura 4:157–59 in a way which fits the meaning of sura 3:55?

We must first decide on the exact meaning of the verbs used in these verses. '*Qatala*' denotes the action of causing someone to die violently ('to put to death', 'to murder'). '*Ṣalaba*' expresses the act of crucifying someone, thus condemning him to a dreadful, shameful death, to make him appear as an odious criminal, and to shame his name for ever. The Jews wanted to subject Jesus to such a death. And they succeeded — apparently. But in fact God saved his servant, clearing his name of guilt and justifying him by raising him from the dead and lifting him up to be with himself. This amazing act of divine intervention threw the Jews into confusion. Once they realized that the tomb was empty, they no longer knew if they had really killed Jesus. So Jesus was not 'really' killed, because God subsequently brought him back to life.

The underlying concept of this interpretation is the same as for the previous one. God does, indeed, give his servants victory over their enemies, but not always in the same way. God's justice has not always spared his prophets from being unjustly put to death. Sura 4:155 states clearly that the Jews had killed many prophets before Jesus. It is Jesus' exceptional rank among the prophets which accounts for God's mighty intervention on his behalf.

The advantage of this interpretation, which goes back to a very early Muslim tradition, is that it enables two apparently contradictory Qur'anic texts to be brought into harmony. Its one weak point is that, at first sight, it does not seem to fit the meaning of sura 4:157–59.

IS THERE ANY FURTHER EVIDENCE?

Many Muslims cling to the dominant interpretation which regards the death of Jesus as occurring just before the Day of Resurrection — and they are perfectly entitled to their view.

Others, recognizing the difficulty of choosing between the two interpretations, admit frankly that the Qur'an's teaching on the death of Jesus is, to say the least, problematic. The question which then arises is this: in such situations, may we turn to sources of evidence *other than* the Qur'an which may throw light on the problem? Each Muslim must answer that question for himself.

If the answer were 'yes', we should have to look at two sources above all others — the testimony of historians, and the testimony of the Bible.

All the historians who make any reference to Jesus are unanimous. These men were not Christians, and Jesus was not important to them. This only serves to make their accounts all the more valuable . . . and every one of them states that Jesus died.[37]

The Gospel records of Jesus' suffering and death are remarkable for their vivid narrative and for the disproportionate amount of space they take up compared to the Gospels' account of Jesus' public life generally.[38]

Râzî is aware that Christians maintain that some of Jesus' disciples were eyewitnesses of his death[39] and that their accounts, recorded in the Gospel narratives, have been passed on from generation to generation of Christians the world over. He does not dispute that there are many of these convergent testimonies ('*tawâtur*'), or that this gives these writings an authority comparable to that of the Qur'an. But he maintains that because these accounts were written by only a few writers, these men were able to make their false accounts agree together. This is a somewhat surprising explanation coming from such a great commentator on the Qur'an! For if Jesus had not died, and if, as Muslim commentators say, he appeared to his disciples to tell them that he was still alive, there would be no reason for such a lie. After all, the disciples saw their master as a triumphant Messiah and were deeply shocked when Jesus told them of his approaching death.[40] On the other hand, their joy at finding that Jesus has risen[41] is quite understandable, as is their insistence on presenting his resurrection as the main proof that he was the Messiah.[42]

We must also bear in mind that Jesus' disciples were the first to recognize that his resurrection endorsed his claims and showed that God had declared him innocent.[43] In the same way, the writer of the fourth Gospel, one of the eyewitnesses of Jesus' death and resurrection, refers to both events as the 'lifting up' of Jesus, first on the cross and then into heaven after his resurrection.[44] This particular use of the verb 'to lift up' is similar to the use of the same verb in the Qur'an.[45] The real question is whether the Qur'anic meaning is related to the meaning we find in the Gospel.

Both these sources, then, confirm the plausibility of the interpretation which Muslim tradition has kept in the background. In the end it is up to each individual Muslim to decide whether his faith can accept it or not.

THE MEANING OF JESUS' DEATH FROM A CHRISTIAN PERSPECTIVE

Jesus' death was certainly caused by his contemporaries' refusal to have their traditions challenged. These traditions were originally meant to clarify and apply the Word of God; instead, they ended up by taking its place.[46] But, over and above the historical circumstances, Jesus' death fulfils God's eternal plan of salvation for mankind. In fact, his death is the logical outcome of God's ongoing self-revelation.

Three distinct aspects of the Law of Moses can be seen in Jesus' death. Firstly, there is the ceremonial law, such as the sacrificial system which symbolizes the need for an expiatory sacrifice for the forgiveness of sins. Secondly, there is the moral law, summed up in the Ten Commandments which spell out the kind of life which God intends mankind to follow. Thirdly, there is the spiritual law, which nourishes the believer's spiritual life and sustains him as he awaits the coming of the Messiah, and as he reads all the prophecies about him.

The moral law is like a schoolteacher,[47] in two ways: it teaches mankind how to live according to God's will and so, at the same time, makes us aware of all our failings.[48] Its purpose, therefore, is to awaken in mankind a sense of our deep need both of God's liberating forgiveness and of his power to save and regenerate us.[49]

This is where Jesus comes in: he is in fact the promised Messiah and his death is the sacrifice for sin which enables God to grant us his forgiveness. The resurrection of Jesus shows that God accepted this sacrifice[50] and, because of it, God acquits us while still being a just judge.[51] The good news of the gospel is that, instead of condemning us according to his justice, God acquits us through the sacrifice of Jesus Christ.

So, anyone who believes in Jesus as the Christ receives

from God the forgiveness of their sins. God's Spirit then comes to live in him, makes him into a new person, sanctifies them and gives them the strength to do God's will. A Christian's good deeds are nothing for him to be proud of: they are simply the result of the Holy Spirit acting within that person. In fact, if that person did *not* do good deeds we would have reason to think that his faith was not genuine.[52] The Christian wants to do good, not in order to win God's approval but in order to express his gratitude to God for the loving kindness and mercy which God has shown to him in the person of Jesus Christ.[53]

So, then, salvation is founded on Jesus' redeeming death;[54] it is continually being worked out in the life of the Christian,[55] and it will be completed and clearly displayed at the Last Judgment.[56] At the Last Judgment, each person will be judged according to what he has done. God himself, of course, is the one who has been producing in believers good works which are evidence of the faith whereby they are saved. This is why the Christian view can be summed up in the apparently paradoxical statement: 'Judgment according to deeds; salvation by faith in Jesus Christ.'

The background to the Christian interpretation of Jesus' death is the biblical concept of sin. Because of the covenant between God and Adam, the whole human race shares the sin of its forefather. We are born into sin even though we are fully responsible only for our own sins. As leader of a new human race, Jesus Christ is the new Adam who rescues mankind from the death into which the first Adam's sin had led them. Those who now enter into the *new* covenant, which has been made possible by Jesus Christ, share in the life of the risen Christ. So Christianity is not a legal code to be observed but a life received, which is constantly flowing out in the service of God and of our fellow human beings.

There are clear reasons why Islam has no concept of sacrifice as a means of obtaining forgiveness for sins.[57]

According to the Qur'an, man's soul is prone to evil,[58] but evil is not inherent in human nature. Adam repented of his disobedience and God forgave him.[59] Consequently, no one is born into sin: people become sinners by disobeying God's Law. Anyone can follow the straight path provided God guides him to it[60] and God's spirit strengthens him.[61] If he strays from it he should repent and trust to God's mercy for the forgiveness of his sins.[62] At the Last Judgment he will be saved if his good deeds outweigh his bad deeds, unless he has committed any really serious sins.

The Islamic principle of judgment according to one's deeds implies that salvation for the Muslim depends largely on whether he has done good and, especially, whether he has practised the Five Pillars of Islam which are the essential expression of his faith in God. A saying attributed to the sixth Shi'a imam, Ğa 'far al-Ṣâdiq, perfectly illustrates the idea that these good deeds are, themselves, the result of God's grace at work in the life of the Muslim:

'Yours be the praise, O God, if I obey you;
Yours too is the right to judge me if I disobey you.
There is no merit either for me or for anyone if I do good;
There is no excuse either for me or for anyone if I do
    evil.'[63]

NOTES

1   Q sura 3 (Al-'Imrân):37–41; sura 19 (Maryam):1–15; sura 21 (Al-Anbiya'):89–90.
2   Q sura 3 (Al-'Imrân):38–39.
3   Q sura 3 (Al-'Imrân):45–46.
4   Q sura 3 (Al-'Imrân):46; sura 5 (Al-Mâ'ida):110; sura 19 (Maryam):16–38.

5   Q sura 21 (Al-Anbiyâ'):91; sura 66 (Al-Taḥrîm):12.
6   Q sura 19 (Maryam):21.
7   Q sura 5 (Al-Mâ'ida):110.
8   Q sura 21 (Al-Anbiyâ'):91.
9   Q sura 3 (Al-'Imrân):48; sura 5 (Al-Mâ'ida):110.
10   Q sura 2 (Al-Baqara):97.
11   Q sura 19 (Maryam):30.
12   Q sura 3 (Al-'Imrân):4; sura 5 (Al-Mâ'ida):46.
13   Q sura 57 (Al-Hadîd):27.
14   Q sura 3 (Al-'Imrân):49.
15   Q sura 43 (Al-Zukhruf):57, 59.
16   Q sura 19 (Maryam):31.
17   Q sura 3 (Al-'Imrân):50; sura 19 (Maryam):36; sura 43 (Al-Zukhruf):64.
18   Q sura 3 (Al-'Imrân):50.
19   Q sura 2 (Al-Baqara):87, 253; sura 5 (Al-Mâ'ida):110.
20   Q sura 5 (Al-Mâ'ida):110; sura 3 (Al-'Imrân):49.
21   Q sura 43 (Al-Zukhruf):63; sura 61 (Al-Ṣaff):6.
22   Q sura 61 (Al-Ṣaff):14.
23   Q sura 3 (Al-'Imrân):54.
24   Q sura 19 (Maryam):33.
25   Q sura 19 (Maryam):15.
26   Q sura 5 (Al-Mâ'ida):116 and 117.
27   Q sura 4 (Al-Nisâ'):96; sura 6 (Al-An'âm):60–61; sura 39 (Al-Zumar):42.
28   Q sura 3 (Al-'Imrân):55.
29   See Râzî, *al-Tafsîr al-Kabîr* on Qur'an sura 3:55.
30   Q sura 4 (Al-Nisâ'):157–59.
31   See Râzî, *al-Tafsîr al-Kabîr* on Qur'an sura 4:157–59.
32   See Ṭabarî, *al-Tafsîr* on Qur'an sura 3:55.
33   Q sura 22 (Al-Ḥajj):40.
34   Q sura 21 (Al-Anbiyâ'):51–77.
35   Q sura 28 (Al-Qasâs):18–28.
36   See L. Massignon, *Opera Minora* (Beirut: Dar al-ma'ârif, 1963), t.2, pp. 534–36. Bearing in mind that the traditional opinion on this matter has not been shared by all Muslim thinkers, the author cites the names of three Ismâ'îlî philosophers and theologians who believed that when Jesus' body died, his divine soul rose to God (Iḫwân al-Ṣafâ, Abû

Hâtim Râzî, Mu'ayyad Šîrâzî). The same belief is expressed in Šahrastânî's chapter on the Shi'ite faith in his well-known work, *al-fiṣal wa-l-niḥal* (Cairo, 1968). The author relates that a number of imamite sects did not believe that their imams really died. The sixth imam, who died in the year 148/765, is said to have explicitly likened his son's fate to that of Jesus.

37 For example, the testimony of Flavius Josephus (first-century Jewish historian) in his *Antiquities of the Jews* and that of Tacitus (Roman historian, early second century).

38 NT Matthew 26, 27; Mark 14, 15; Luke 22, 23; John 18, 19.

39 NT Matthew 27:55–56; Mark 15:40–41; Luke 23:49–55; John 19:25,27.

40 NT Matthew 16:21–23; Mark 14:26–31; Luke 22:31–34; John 13:36–38; 18:10–11.

41 NT Luke 24:36–43; John 20:19–20.

42 NT Acts 2:22–36; 13:26–37.

43 NT Acts 2:36; Romans 1:4; 1 Timothy 3:16.

44 NT John 12:31–33.

45 Q sura 4 (Al-Nisâ'):157–58.

46 NT Mark 7:1–23.

47 NT Galatians 3:24.

48 NT Romans 7:7–25.

49 NT Romans 8:1–4.

50 NT Romans 4:25.

51 NT Romans 3:26.

52 NT James 2:14–26.

53 NT Ephesians 2:8–10.

54 NT Romans 3:21–26.

55 NT Ephesians 3:20; Philippians 2:12.

56 NT Romans 8:24; 1 Peter 1:15.

57 Nevertheless, the concept of ransom does occur at least once in the Qur'an. In the account of the sacrifice of Abraham's son (who is not named in the passage) God states that he has ransomed the child 'with a noble sacrifice' (sura 37:107).

58 Q sura 12 (Yûsuf):53.

59 Q sura 2 (Al-Baqara):37.

60 Q sura 1 (Al-Fâtiha):6.

61   Q sura 58 (Al-Mujâdila):22.
62   Q sura 15 (Al-Ḥijr):56; sura 39 (Al-Zumar):53; sura 42 (Al-Shûra):28.
63   Quoted by Šahrastânî *al-milal-wa-l-nîḥal*, vol. 1, ch.6, 'the imamites'.

6

JESUS CHRIST: SON OF GOD?

The beginning of the last chapter gave a general description of Jesus from the Qur'an. We need to look again at that picture so as to understand the meaning of the terms in which the Qur'an describes Jesus and to see more clearly the nature of the disagreement about Jesus' person between Christians and Muslims.[1]

JESUS' NAME AND ATTRIBUTES

Jesus, son of Mary

The name which is given most frequently (twenty-five times) to Jesus in the Qur'an is 'Îsâ. The most likely explanation of its derivation is that it comes from the name Esau. Possibly Esau's name was applied to Jesus because the Jews, who despised Jacob's twin brother, were also hostile to Jesus. Muhammad may well, therefore, have heard the name used by Arab Jews but been unaware of its pejorative connotations.

The name Jesus itself comes from the Hebrew 'Yeshua' via the Greek 'Iésous', and it means 'God saves'. Matthew 1:21 states: 'he will save his people from their sins'. Islam, which defines God's relationship with mankind in terms of 'guidance', obviously does not recognize Jesus' exclusive role as Saviour as it is presented in the New Testament.[2]

In the Qur'an Jesus is called 'son of Mary' thirty-three times and on sixteen of these occasions he is called 'Jesus, son of Mary'. Only once is this name applied to him in the Gospels.[3] This way of referring to Jesus may be connected with the important position given to Mary in some seventh-century Christian circles. It is significant in another way too; the Arab custom at that time was to name a person according to his line of descent on his father's side. So, to call Jesus 'son of Mary' stresses the extraordinary fact of his having been born without a father, but it may also reflect Muslim-Christian controversy about him: Jesus, the son of Mary, is not the Son of God as Christians say he is.[4] He was born like any other human being, born of a woman although by miraculous conception.

Jesus, the Word and Spirit of God

The Qur'an's accounts of the Annunciation[5] have many similarities, and as many dissimilarities, with the Gospel accounts.[6] These two titles, 'word' and 'spirit', which are given to Jesus in the Qur'an[7] are interpreted in various ways by Muslim commentators.

The first title, which occurs three times in the Qur'an, is understood in the light of Jesus' miraculous birth. Mary, startled at the news which the angels have brought her, asks them a question[8] to which she is given a clear answer: nothing is impossible for God. He has only to speak a word to call into being whoever he wishes.[9] That is how he created Adam, who had neither father nor mother.[10] In this sense, Jesus is the fulfilment of God's creative Word,[11] but he can also be called God's Word in a broader sense. He fulfils the word spoken by earlier prophets, he speaks God's word in his own capacity as prophet, and, again, he may be thought of as the incarnation of the good news announced to Mary.[12]

For Christians, Jesus is God's Word in a similar kind of way to that in which Muslims consider the Qur'an to be

God's word. His place in Christianity is very similar to the place of the Qur'an in Islam. The Qur'an, although it is God's eternal word, becomes 'incarnate' on the pages where it is written or in the mouth of someone reading it: yet its message nonetheless remains eternal. In a similar way, the eternal Word of God, revealed to his prophets, was fully revealed in Jesus Christ. As a descendant of Adam,[13] Jesus is a human being like any other, except that he is without sin.[14] Nevertheless, when the creative Word of God, the expression of his wisdom,[15] joined itself to human nature in the person of Jesus[16], its status as the eternal Word of God was in no way altered. In other words, Jesus is the incarnation of the eternal, creative and personal Word of God.

The title 'spirit of God' which the Qur'an gives to Jesus is connected, by Muslim commentators, either with the angel Gabriel, who appeared to Mary in human form to announce to her the forthcoming birth of her son,[17] or with the spirit of God which was breathed into Mary's womb[18] and which, coupled with God's creative Word, brought Jesus into being. Gabriel is also the holy spirit who strengthened Jesus throughout his life.[19] We should note, however, that the Qur'an makes a distinction between the spirit and the angels.[20]

The Gospels, on the other hand, clearly distinguish between the angel Gabriel and the Holy Spirit, who was in fact God's agent in the conception of Jesus.[21] The Holy Spirit is the Spirit of God who descended upon Jesus at his baptism, in the form of a dove.[22] He was also active throughout Jesus' ministry.[23] Just before he died[24] and shortly after his resurrection,[25] Jesus promised his disciples that he would send them the Holy Spirit after he himself had been lifted up to God. This Holy Spirit is the Spirit of truth whose mission was to give Jesus' disciples full knowledge of Christ and the power to carry his gospel beyond the frontiers of Israel.[26]

Jesus the Messiah

This title appears eleven times in the Qur'an, including one of the Annunciation passages.[27] Muslim commentators have, in general, recognized the origin of the word 'Messiah', meaning 'Anointed One', but they have interpreted this 'anointing' in various ways.

Ṭabarî believes that Jesus received from Gabriel an anointing which preserved him from the evil which the devil inflicts on human beings from the time they are born.[28] Thus the angel told Mary that a holy boy would be born to her.[29] But this anointing is also understood in the sense of a special blessing which Jesus received from God. This blessing would account for the fact that Jesus, a righteous man,[30] was blessed wherever he might be.[31] In the active sense, Jesus is the Messiah because he anointed the eyes of the blind with a holy oil, because he laid his hands on the sick to heal them, and because he cleansed men from their sins. There is, too, a somewhat mystical interpretation which traces the word 'Messiah' to the root word '*sâḥa*', meaning 'to wander'. According to this view, Jesus was called the Messiah because of his life of constant pilgrimage or wandering.[32]

In the biblical context the Messiah is the king whom God promised he would raise up as a descendant of David.[33] Solomon, for all the greatness and prosperity of his kingdom, was only a pale foreshadowing of the Messiah. This king would enjoy a father-son relationship with God and would make all the peoples of the earth his subjects.[34] Yet David himself called him his Lord.[35] The prophet Micah identified Bethlehem as the place where the Messiah would be born and described his origins as ancient and eternal.[36] Isaiah gave him the name Emmanuel (God with us) and predicted that his birth would be miraculous.[37] This new-born king would preside over an eternal kingdom of peace and justice.[38] In view of all this it is hardly surprising that, in the few centuries before Jesus' birth, many people were eagerly awaiting the coming of the Messiah. However, since the Jews were by then under the domination of the Romans, their messianic hope had taken on a basically political emphasis.

The Gospel genealogies present Jesus as the son of David.[39] The angel Gabriel tells Mary that her son will sit on the throne of David, his father.[40] And Jesus was born in Bethlehem, the town of David.[41] Some thirty years later, Jesus' disciples gradually discover that their master is, in fact, the Christ,[42] which is our English translation, via the Greek, of the word 'Messiah'. Jesus himself states that he is the Messiah.[43] Nevertheless he refuses to be crowned king by a crowd of people who are amazed by his miracles.[44] Before Jesus sets off for Jerusalem, where he knows he will be crucified, his disciples become finally convinced that he is the Messiah, but to avoid any popular misunderstanding he asks them not to tell anyone of his Messiahship.[45] When interrogated by the religious authorities, Jesus says that he is not the sort of Messiah his fellow-countrymen were expecting, as he does not want to be mistaken for a political king. But he declares that he certainly is the Messiah foretold by the prophets.[46] When the Roman governor asks him whether he is, indeed, the King of the Jews, Jesus replies that his heavenly kingdom is not to be identified with any earthly political kingdom.[47] In the end Jesus is condemned to death for his messianic claims, and he dies on a cross which bears the inscription: 'Jesus of Nazareth, the King of the Jews'.[48]

The resurrection of Jesus is his real enthronement as Messiah.[49] Since his ascension to God he reigns as king over all those who confess that he is the Christ, until the day when his Messiahship is recognized by the whole world — the day when he returns in glory.[50]

Jesus, God's prophet, apostle and servant
The Qur'an places Jesus in a line of prophets, the most

famous of whom are Adam, Noah, Abraham, Moses, Jesus and Muhammad, the latter being the 'Seal' of them all.[51] According to the Qur'an, soon after Jesus was born he announced that he was God's servant and prophet.[52] The angel Gabriel had told Mary that her son would be an apostle of God.[53] Muslim writers distinguish between 'apostle' and 'prophet', in that all prophets proclaim God's oneness and call their peoples to be subject to him, whereas only apostles are instructed to bring their people a Law. Between Moses and Muhammad, therefore, Jesus introduced a Law which modified the Law of Moses and prepared the way for the Law of Islam. Like Moses before him, Jesus was sent to the children of Israel,[54] even though both the Torah and the gospel are a guidance for mankind,[55] especially for those who fear God.[56] The miraculous birth of Jesus,[57] his speech from the cradle[58] and the miracles he performed are all signs confirming his apostleship.[59] The fact remains, however, that Jesus is only one of several servants of God,[60] and this implies that the Messiah, like the angels, is simply a created being who is obedient to God.[61]

The Bible also presents Jesus as a prophet, an apostle and a servant of God, but in quite a different sense.

Moses had told his people that God would raise up for them a prophet like himself.[62] On the basis of this prophecy, the Jews were waiting for the arrival of a prophet of Moses' stature, whom they identified with the Messiah. They were still waiting for this prophet when Jesus started preaching. Some of them asked John the Baptist if he was the expected prophet,[63] but John firmly denied it and drew his questioners' attention to Jesus.[64] Seeing the miracles Jesus did[65] and hearing his words,[66] a number of Jews believed that he was the Prophet whose coming had been foretold by Moses, while others believed he was just one of the prophets.[67] God attested that Jesus was, indeed, the Prophet.[68] Jesus himself came to the Jews who did not believe in him as the Prophet spoken of by Moses.[69] After Jesus' resurrection, his disciples announced that their master was the 'new Moses',[70] just as they had originally believed.[71] Moses was indeed a 'prefiguring' of Jesus in the sense that he was God's prophet, the leader and liberator of his people who, despite his miracles, opposed him.

John's Gospel presents Jesus as the apostle sent into the world by God, not to condemn it but to save it.[72] He does what God does,[73] speaks God's words and is filled with his Spirit.[74] His mission is to unite his people with God just as intimately as he himself is united with God, so that the world may recognize that God has sent him.[75] In fact, eternal life consists in knowing God and the one he sent.[76] This apostle of God comes from God[77] and returns to him,[78] after having loved his own people enough to give up his own life for them.[79]

In the book of the prophet Isaiah we find God's Servant described in four portraits which have become known as the 'Servant Songs'.

The first of these describes the Servant as God's chosen one in whom he delights. Upheld by God and empowered by his Spirit, his mission is to bring justice to the nations. He carries out his mission peacefully, resolutely and yet with great compassion for those who are weak and faltering. Like Moses, he brings in a new covenant between God and Man and a new Law: but, unlike Moses, he brings light not only to Israel but to all the peoples of the earth.[80]

The second Song confirms the universal character of the Servant's mission. Called by God from the moment he was born, he enjoys a special relationship with him. Rejected by Israel, he is the initiator of a salvation which only a part of the people of Israel receives, along with the other nations of the earth. And so he brings glory to God and is himself glorified by him.[81]

The third Servant Song depicts him as the perfect

disciple, who listens to God's word and communicates it to mankind. Condemned by men, he is justified by God. His word is the word of God, comforting those who place their trust in him and judging those who rebel.[82]

The last Song shows the Servant as both victim and conqueror of man's sin. Humiliated by men, and put to death by them, he prays to God for them. So God accepts that the violent death of his Servant should be an atoning sacrifice for all nations. For having freely given up his life as a sacrifice, the Servant will himself be raised to life again, exalted and honoured by God. He will be given, as descendants, a vast multitude of human beings who will be justified by him if they recognize what he has done.[83]

John the Baptist points to Jesus as the Lamb of God who takes away the sin of the world.[84] From the time of his baptism Jesus receives God's witness that he is the chosen Servant.[85] Jesus, then, sees his own mission as fulfilling that of the Servant of the Old Testament.[86] His death is the seal of the new covenant which makes forgiveness of sins available to the whole human race.[87] Jesus' disciples recognize in their master the humble and compassionate Servant of God, who is made the object of Israel's hostility.[88] Their preaching was based on the certainty that Isaiah's prophecies about the Servant had been fulfilled in the person of Jesus, the Christ,[89] and this conviction can be seen in all their writings.[90]

To sum up, then: the various titles which the Qur'an gives to Jesus show clearly that he has a prominent position among the prophets. No doubt this explains why he is referred to as 'noble in this world and in the next',[91] as Moses was to some degree.[92] So Jesus is not only honoured by men: his supremacy derives from his special relationship with God. Like the angels[93] he is 'near to God'.[94] God's special favour and sovereign mercy bestowed on Jesus[95] show that God exalts some prophets above others.[96] God's favour is the result of his sovereign grace and mercy.[97]

Nevertheless, this difference in rank does not make Jesus essentially any different from the other prophets. The honour given to Jesus in the Qur'an is certainly the reason why he has exerted such a fascination over Muslim mystics. This is true, for example, of the famous Muslim mystic philosopher Ibn 'Arabî (560/1165-638/1240) who, comparing Jesus with Muhammad, calls Jesus 'the seal of the saints'.[98]

The titles of Prophet, Apostle and Servant given to Jesus in the Gospels do not simply show that God had a special love for Jesus; they point to the unique position he holds which makes him unlike any other prophet. And that is something we shall be examining more closely.

JESUS, PROPHET OF MONOTHEISM

We know that Muhammad's mission was to preach God's oneness to the Arabs who used to associate many gods with the supreme God. Because God is one, mankind should worship only the Creator and be subject to his will alone.[99] The 'associationism' of the Arabs was such that they believed God to have relations: a wife or wives, sons and daughters.[100] The Qur'an even records the names of the three principal goddesses who were worshipped in pre-Islamic religion.[101] This goddess-worship was all the more blasphemous given the way in which the Arabs of that time treated women. The Qur'an's strong attack upon Arab polytheism was, therefore, intended to preserve God's transcendence and to prevent any deification of his creatures,[102] who would then become a part of God himself.[103] So the unforgivable sin, according to the Qur'an, is to include created beings in the worship which is due to the Creator.[104]

It is against this background of Muhammad's intense struggle against Arab polytheism that we must understand his opposition to Christians, who were similarly accused of 'associationism'. It is with the same anti-polytheistic energy and enthusiasm that Muhammad denounces the Christian claim that the Messiah is the Son of God,[105] and that God is the Messiah.[106] With even greater justification he refutes their allegation that God is the third member of a triad[107] composed of God, Mary and Jesus.[108] Jesus himself, on the other hand, is held blameless by the Qur'an, which predicts that he will speak out against the Christians because they have deified him[109] and presents him as a monotheistic prophet faithful to the mission which God entrusted to him.[110]

These accusations levelled against Christians are not without some historical basis. Church history indeed shows that Christians have not always been monotheists beyond reproach! If all Christian Arabs of Muhammad's time had kept strictly to their master's teaching, they would, perhaps, not have been so severely criticized by the Qur'an. Their beliefs and practices concerning the divinity of Christ and the holy trinity, such as are referred to and rightly condemned in the Qur'an, perfectly illustrate the serious departures from Christian truth of which those particular Christians were guilty. Their tritheism is completely foreign to biblical teaching. The same is true of their representation of Christ's divinity in terms of earthly sonship beginning from the moment of Jesus' conception in his mother's womb. Their worship of monks and other religious leaders as well as Christ[111] is in open opposition to the teaching of Jesus.[112] This religious confusion certainly did nothing to clarify the position occupied by Jesus in authentic Christianity.

JESUS AND GOD

In the Gospels we read that Jesus, before beginning his ministry, spent forty days in the desert. After this long period of fasting we see the devil challenging Jesus to prove to him that he is the Son of God. Jesus refuses the challenge and, faithful to the message preached by all the prophets, asserts the oneness of God and his exclusive right to be worshipped by men.[113] In his public life Jesus never hesitates to declare himself a human being in the full sense of the word.[114] Like all human beings, he experiences tiredness, hunger and thirst[115] and he weeps over the death of a friend.[116] Gentle and humble in heart,[117] he makes friends with very ordinary people and even with social outcasts. His relationship with God seems nothing unusual, except that he spends whole nights praying. He does not lay claim to divine goodness,[118] he states that God is greater than he is[119] and he willingly admits his own ignorance of some things which only God knows.[120] He refers to himself most frequently as the 'Son of man', a title which, more than any other, underlines his humanity. It is on the night before his death that Jesus' humanity is seen most clearly, when he begs God to save him, if possible, from the suffering he is about to face. Yet — and this is to be noted — he also knows that it is for this very purpose that he has come, and he declares his resolve to glorify, above all, the name of the One who has sent him.[121]

In this light, then, we see Jesus as a perfect 'Muslim' (in the sense that he is totally submitted to God). But the Gospel records also cast another light on him, clarifying our view of him. At the start of his mission we see Jesus publicly receiving God's testimony that he is his Son.[122] Jesus never draws attention to this title, so as not to jeopardize God's oneness in the minds of those who are unprepared for this revelation. On the other hand, he behaves in ways entirely consistent with his divine origin. In his preaching he states that the kingdom of God, which he has been sent to establish on earth, is near at hand and he calls his fellow men to repent so that they may enter the Kingdom.[123] The miracles he performs, particularly to help the most helpless people, are the signs pointing forward to the coming Kingdom. The crowds are astounded by the exceptional authority with which Jesus teaches.[124] He forgives a paralyzed man his sins and then gives him the power to walk again in order to show those who were outraged at his behaviour that he has the authority to do this.[125] He accepts worship from a repentant sinner.[126] Occasionally he states openly that he is the Son of God and thus also the Son of man whom God has appointed as supreme judge of all men.[127] The Jewish leaders, challenged to prove him guilty,[128] realize that Jesus is implicitly claiming to be God.[129] From that day on, they try to find a suitable opportunity to arrest him[130] because they are afraid of how his mass of followers will react to his arrest.[131] When eventually they manage to lay hands on him, they subject him to an interrogation and accuse him of having claimed to be God's Son.[132] Jesus does not deny what he has said, but he points out that this is in line with divine revelation and in no way detracts from the oneness of God. And so the result is that Jesus is condemned as a blasphemer for having claimed to be the Messiah and the Son of God.[133]

Jesus' relationship with his disciples is quite different. First, they become aware of their master's holiness[134] and are amazed at his power over the forces of nature.[135] Jesus reveals to them that he is the Son of God;[136] and little by little they discover the truth of these words.[137] Jesus' unique relationship with his Father exemplifies his disciples' relationship with God.[138] The risen Jesus appears to his disciples in his divine glory. He sends them out to the four corners of the earth, promising them his continuing presence and unfailing power:

'All authority in heaven and on earth has been given to me. Therefore go and make disciples of all nations, baptizing them in the name of the Father and of the Son and of the Holy Spirit, and teaching them to obey everything I have commanded you. And surely I will be with you always, to the very end of the age.'[139]

FURTHER THEOLOGICAL POINTS

These two complementary aspects of Jesus are found throughout the Gospels. His disciples become more and more aware of them as they get to know him better. And so, with the help of the Holy Spirit which Jesus has promised them, they try to integrate the two views harmoniously into their overall grasp of the mystery of Christ. The writings of the apostles bear unanimous witness that the one and only eternal Son of God became incarnate in the person of Jesus.[140] The Holy Spirit is the eternal Spirit of God whose mission is to reveal the Son to mankind.[141] The Son, who is the perfect image of the invisible God,[142] makes the Father known to them.[143] The Fatherhood of God, the Sonship of Jesus Christ, and the procession of the Holy Spirit define the eternal relationships between the three persons of the Godhead. But this divine tri-unity does not mean that God is One and Three from the same point of view, since this would be a contradiction in terms. God is one in essence, but three in persons. This concept of God consequently rules out the possibility of placing any created being on an equal footing with God.

The trinitarian monotheism of the Bible is radically opposed to the tritheism denounced in the Qur'an. Jesus is not the Son of God in the sense that God begat a human child in Mary's womb, albeit miraculously. God did indeed give Jesus his human nature by means of this conception, and this does make him human in the full sense of the term, justifying his Qur'anic title 'son of Mary'. But this is quite distinct from his divine sonship. He is his mother's son in a purely bodily and earthly way (miraculous though his conception was), but he is the eternal Son of God by virtue of the unique and spiritual relationship which unites God the Father and God the Son. There is a very real difference between the oneness of God's nature and the 'threeness' of his persons, just as there is a very real distinction between 'begetting' in the human sense and 'fatherhood' in the divine sense. That is why it is vital to maintain, as the famous Qur'anic verse does, that 'God does not beget nor is he begotten'.[144] On the other hand, despite these important distinctions, the Bible teaches that the Father 'begets' the Son, the 'only begotten Son' of the Father. To confess that Jesus is the incarnate Son of God is not at all the same thing as making a man into a god, because the incarnation of the Son of God is exactly the opposite of the deification of the man Jesus. The union of the divine and human natures in the single person of Jesus neither deifies human nature nor humanizes divine nature, and thus alters neither of them. According to the biblical conception of God, Jesus is the second person of the divine trinity of Father, Son and Holy Spirit, and not the third after God and Mary. Nor can God be reduced to the person of the Son alone. This is why it is correct to say that Christ is God, but incorrect to say that God is Christ.

OBJECTIONS

Muslim thinkers who have read the Gospel or who have come into contact with orthodox Christians have realized that the tritheism rejected by the Qur'an is not the same thing as the Christian doctrine of Christ's divinity. Their rejection of this doctrine was certainly motivated by the Qur'anic monotheism which had profoundly shaped their thinking, but it could not be based directly on the Qur'an, which knows nothing of this doctrine. Those who have not accused Christians of falsifying the *text* of the Scriptures but its *meaning* only have tried to interpret them in a way which fits the image of the Christ they have derived from the Qur'an. Ġazâlî's apologetic treatise *An excellent refutation of the divinity of Jesus, based on the Gospels* is a perfect example of this.[145]

1. The author deliberately chooses to base his arguments on the Gospel of John, so as better to refute the Christian belief in Christ's divinity, since it is based particularly on this Gospel. He judiciously selects a large number of verses which point to Jesus' humanity,[146] especially his dying words, 'My God, my God, why have you forsaken me?'[147] He then sets these against Christian doctrine and concludes that God cannot possibly have been subjected to the conditions of human life and to death, which is the greatest of life's miseries. Christians, of course, are aware of these verses, from which they recognize that Jesus Christ is not only truly God but also truly human. By becoming a man, the Son of God took on the human condition so completely that he gave up some of his divine privileges in order better to identify with mankind. But the main thrust of Ġazâlî's argument consists in showing how the divinity of Jesus leads to an insoluble problem — the suffering, death and burial of God. He knows that Christians do not claim to have an explanation for everything, but as far as he is concerned, this is further proof that their faith is inconsistent. However, it is worth pointing out that it was not Christ's *nature* which died but his *person*, and that death is not the extinction of the person but its passing from one form of life to another. The fact remains that Jesus feared death all the more because as Son of God he was the source of life and, because of the uniqueness of his death, he was indeed forsaken by the Father at the terrible moment when he was atoning for the sin of the world. So it was not God, as such, who died but the person of his Son.

2. Referring to the verses which present Jesus as the Son of God, the author argues that they must be taken metaphorically. Otherwise they would blatantly contradict reason. In the same way, Jesus' statements about his divinity must be understood in a broad sense. Did not God tell Moses that he would be like God to his brother Aaron?[148] And did he not call men 'gods' in another passage?[149]

If men could be called 'gods' in this way, how much more so the man whom God set apart and sent? As a prophet, Jesus was a god, and being a prophet means much more than being someone to whom God's word is sent, as it was to all Jews. The Jews thus misunderstood the implication of Jesus' words when they accused him of blasphemy.[150] Ġazâlî's interpretation understands the general direction of Jesus' teaching but does not grasp its full implication. In fact Jesus is denouncing the antithesis between Creator and creatures by which the Jews drew a sharp distinction between God and men. From the fact that men are called 'gods' in Psalm 82, Jesus was arguing that the incarnation of the Son of God is theologically consistent. This incarnation perfectly accomplishes God's declared intention to reveal himself to his creatures. Jesus is not merely identifying himself with the people to whom God's word was addressed, he is not only the one sent by God; he is also showing that he is superior to those people because he is also the eternal Son of God who introduces them to his Father so that God can become *their* Father[151] — by adoption. In this connection it is noteworthy that Jesus never associates himself with his disciples in calling God 'Our Father'. He always says either 'my Father' or 'your Father' or simply 'the Father'.

3. A second passage discussed by Ġazâlî in order to refute the divinity of Jesus is the one which portrays the disciples as united to God in the same way that Jesus is united to his

Father.[152] The author comments that if this union implies the divinity of Jesus, then it also implies the deification of his disciples. But, as the author quite rightly points out, the disciples spoke of their union with God without ever claiming divinity for themselves.[153] Yet their writings testify both to Jesus' humanity and to his divinity.[154] In fact, Christ's union with his Father, which is the model for his disciples' union with God, does not necessarily entail deifying those disciples any more than Jesus' human nature is deified by its union with his divine nature. The personal union between Christians and God, brought about by the presence of the Holy Spirit within them, is like the union of Christ's two natures, i.e. the distinct persons involved are neither confused one with another nor is either of them transformed.

4. Gazâlî also examines Jesus' argument with the Jews, in the course of which he states that he existed before Abraham.[155] We must agree with the author that the patriarch Abraham received a revelation concerning the coming of Jesus; but we can hardly go along with Gazâlî when he interprets Jesus' existence before Abraham as meaning merely that God had decreed, in eternity, that he would send his messenger. This explanation ignores the real meaning of Jesus' words: 'before Abraham was born, I AM!' Here, as elsewhere in this Gospel, Jesus calls himself by the very name of God which was revealed to Moses.[156] Similarly, Gazâlî takes Jesus' reply to Philip[157] to mean that Jesus is simply God's representative, whereas in fact it goes much further than that. Jesus had been clearly teaching that he was greater than the prophets; because they were God's servants, whereas he was God's Son and heir.[158] In John chapter 14 he declares his perfect identity with the Father who has sent him ('Anyone who has seen me has seen the Father'). He says that after he has returned to the Father, the Holy Spirit will be given to his

disciples, enabling them to extend the Christian community which he had founded within the People of Israel, to all the peoples of the world. He assures them that, in so doing, they will do greater deeds than his own.

5. The passage which Ġazâlî really had to discuss is, of course, the beginning of John's Gospel which, in terms reminiscent of the beginning of Genesis, describes Jesus as the divine *Logos*.[159] Christian Arabs who had clung to a sound doctrine of God's tri-unity did in fact make use of this particular passage to present to Muslims the three persons of the one divine essence, and did so using philosophical categories which could not but hold the attention of any writer seeking an understanding of the faith. The Father is pure Intelligence, the Son is Intelligence in action and the Holy Spirit is self-aware Intelligence. This is not the place to go into this highly technical argument, but suffice it to say that Ġazâlî's view is severely challenged by this lucid formulation of the doctrine of the Trinity. Let us note in passing that Christians, basing their view on the revelation that God is Love,[160] had also likened the Holy Spirit to the bond of love between the Father and the Son.

6. Ġazâlî is right to stress that Jesus is not the only prophet to have performed miracles. Moses and other later prophets did so too. And it is true that it is not Jesus' miracles which, ultimately, distinguish him from God's other messengers. However, some of the Gospel accounts show Jesus acting in a way in which only God is entitled to act (for example, forgiving people's sins, and accepting their worship), and ascribing to himself qualities which are God's alone (such as holiness, judgment, omnipresence and omnipotence). Ġazâlî pays hardly any attention to these accounts. He nevertheless recognizes that Jesus is the only prophet to have called himself Son of God, God

and Lord. Ġazâlî justifies Jesus' exclusive right to use such metaphorical language by the fact that Jesus is the founder of a Law. But why, in that case, was the privilege not rather accorded to Muhammad who, in the Muslim view, was the last of the prophets and was given the task of setting up a perfect and definitive Law among men? On the other hand, says Ġazâlî, metaphorical language must be correctly interpreted. Thus, to call God 'Father' is, he says, a way of reminding ourselves of God's care, mercy and kindness towards mankind;[161] to call oneself the Son of God is just a way of stating one's respect for God and one's submission to his will;[162] to speak of the Spirit of God is to refer to the grace, the blessings and the protection with which God surrounds his creatures. This minimalist interpretation by Ġazâlî of scriptural passages is intended to reduce Jesus' union with God to a merely moral level. But if this really was what Jesus meant by those words, why did he not make an effort to clear up the misunderstanding in the minds of his enemies when they sentenced him for blasphemy? When he appears before the Jewish court, we in fact find him repeating his earlier claims to be God. It is also noteworthy that Ġazâlî's interpretation is thoroughly rationalistic. This rationalism, which appears throughout his work, is all the more surprising coming from a theologian who represents Muslim orthodoxy, which accepts the principle that faith may deal with matters beyond the grasp of human reason. This is the case, for example, with verses in the Qur'an which depict God in anthropomorphic language. Sunni theology accepts that this language describes reality, but recognizes — given that God is spirit and not a body — that what it describes is inexplicable.

However, Ġazâlî's view is also based on theological assumptions which are peculiar to Muslim teaching. The absolute transcendence of God, which is central to Muslim theology, makes it impossible to conceive that God could become incarnate in human form. God's justice and majesty are felt to be seriously threatened if the consequences of human sin are borne by God. His immutability is such that God cannot experience human reality. Christian theology also stresses the radical transcendence of God and his perfect justice. Nevertheless, it bases the incarnation of the Son of God on the all-powerful sovereignty of God, on his infinite love, on his strong desire to reveal himself to the highest of his creatures and on the reality of God's relationship to history. These principles are not entirely foreign to the Qur'anic revelation, but Muslim theology did not develop them in the same way.

SINGULAR OR PLURAL MONOTHEISM?

Singular monotheism, forcefully proclaimed by the Qur'an holds an understandable fascination for the human mind. But it cannot avoid being threatened by certain dangers which arise from the fact that the concept of God in any religion naturally determines its view of his relationship to the created world.

Monotheism establishes, of course, the sovereignty of God as well as the total dependence of the universe on him. But how can the universe be recognized as having a real existence unless the principle of 'otherness' within the Creator is acknowledged? Singular monotheism, which rejects this principle, is therefore immediately open to the danger of a kind of fusional spiritualism. It is well known that some Muslim mystics, seeking an intimate communion with God, crossed the dividing line between God and man, and thus jeopardized the divine transcendence. This monotheism also is in danger of becoming a fatalism, holding God responsible for all human actions, good or bad, thus denying man free exercise of responsibility towards God. So the absence of 'otherness' in God leads Muslim faith to waver between an extremist spiritualism, identifying the Creator with his creation, and a blind fatalism, which exalts divine power and reduces faith to its merely vertical dimension.

On the other hand, plural monotheism permits a qualitative distinction between God and man, conferring on man a separate and real identity. Divine plurality allows man to stand before God as a free and responsible being, in the joyful recognition of the One who has created him so. Man's freedom and creativity blossom as they are governed according to the will and wisdom of God, who is their source. Human deeds are the fruit, both of God's power — the total and primary cause — and of man's power — the total but secondary cause. However, evil, which is the absence or non-existence of good, does not originate with God, but man is held responsible when he commits sin. Human freedom, therefore, does not conflict with God's sovereignty, but neither is it confused with it. All the more so as this freedom is enslaved to evil which deeply troubles man's relationship with God. In his great wisdom, God has allowed evil to exist and has gloriously overcome it through the death and resurrection of his son Jesus, thus restoring to man his freedom as God's creature.

Singular monotheism, which denies God's inter-personality, also leads us to ask the question: how can man enter into a personal relationship with God if God does not have a personal relationship with himself? This kind of monotheism consequently makes the concept of any personal relationship with God extremely fragile. The believer thus finds himself in a formal relationship with God instead of a personal relationship with him. So legalism is a constant threat to the Muslim religion, and it often engenders an activism which tames God's power and reduces faith to its merely horizontal dimension.

Fatalism and activism, two degenerate forms of faith,

are the two contrasting dangers threatening Islam. And isn't the history of the Muslim people punctuated by leaps and bounds after long periods of intellectual and spiritual lethargy?

Multi-personal monotheism, implying interpersonal relationships within the Godhead, leads the believer into a relationship as personal as that between the Son of God and his Father. As the image of God created on the model of his uncreated image,[163] Jesus Christ, man is God's partner. He is the partner of the covenant that God has made with mankind in the person of Jesus Christ. The cross of Jesus Christ is the sign of this kind of monotheism which reconciles perfectly the two dimensions of the Christian faith. The person who grasps its message is restored to a filial communion with God who makes him live by his own life among his fellow beings. Plural monotheism is, of course, also exposed to particular dangers. The tritheism attached to the unfortunately famous name of Jean Philoponus (490–570) is one. The deification of man, to be seen particularly in one tradition of the Eastern Church, is another. Islam is constantly challenging Christians to be alert to these dangers which threaten to weaken God's oneness.

CONCLUSION

The Qur'an's rejection of Christ's divinity is really the rejection of a false concept of that divinity which was brought to Muhammad's attention by a number of Christians living in Arabia and the surrounding area. That the true Christian doctrine should have been confused with tritheism is all the more understandable coming from a setting in which a degenerate form of Christianity was found alongside the Arab polytheism that held sway before the coming of Islam. As a skilful iconoclast, the prophet of Islam successfully rid the Arabs of their idols. Was he an anti-trinitarian in the biblical sense of the term? It does not appear so. Having said this, later Muslim thinkers quite clearly opposed the Christian doctrine.

Their judgment was based on the premise that human reason, despite the weakness imposed on it by sin, is capable of grasping, by its own effort, the truth of its Creator. In the Christian view, this truth is inevitably too high above mankind to be grasped by our unaided reason. It therefore includes 'mysteries' which the Scriptures reveal and which can be grasped only by faith. Faith — the act of trusting by which man humbly listens to God's Word — therefore precedes understanding, but the latter, once it has been enlightened, supplements the former. Thus the Christian accepts by faith these mysteries, which are above reason but not opposed to it, before he tries to penetrate them with his intellect and with the help of God's Spirit who revealed them. Muslim doctrine knows nothing of such mysteries, but it does admit that some things are known only by God. For example, the Qur'an does not deny that God could have chosen a son for himself had he wished.[164] One verse which perfectly expresses the monotheistic passion of the Qur'an and the majestic sovereignty of God goes as far as to call the prophet to submit his intelligence to revelation: 'Say: "If the Lord of Mercy had a son, I would be the first to worship him." '[165]

NOTES

1 For this chapter, we refer the reader to M. Hayek, *Le Christ de l'Islam* (Paris, 1959) and H. Michaud, *Jésus selon le Coran* (Neuchâtel, 1960).

2   NT Luke 2:11; John 4:42; Acts 5:31; Philippians 3:20; 2 Peter 1:1.

3   NT Mark 6:3.

4   NT Matthew 11:27; Mark 1:1; Luke 1:35; John 1:18, 34.

5   Q sura 3 (Al-'Imrân):45–47; sura 19 (Maryam):16–21.

6   NT Matthew 1:18–25; Luke 1:26–38.

7   Q sura 3 (Al-'Imrân):45; sura 4 (Al-Nisâ'):171.

8   Q sura 3 (Al-'Imrân):47; sura 19 (Maryam):20.

9   Q sura 3 (Al-'Imrân):47; sura 19 (Maryam):21.

10 Q sura 3 (Al-'Imrân):59.

11 Q sura 16 (Al-Naḥl):40.

12 Cf. *Encyclopaedia of Islam*, 2nd edition, vol. IV (Leiden, 1978), articles on ''Îsâ' and 'Indjîl' by G. C. Anwati.

13 NT Luke 3:38.

14 NT John 8:46; 14:30; Hebrews 2:17; 4:15.

15 OT Proverbs 8:22–31; NT Colossians 1:15.

16 NT John 1:1–14.

17 Q sura 19 (Maryam):17.

18 Q sura 21 (Al-Anbiyâ'):91; sura 66 (Al-Tahrîm):12.

19 Q sura 2 (Al-Baqara):87, 253; sura 5 (Al-Mâ'ida):110.

20 Q sura 70 (Al-Ma'ârij):4; sura 78 (Al-Naba'):38; sura 97 (Qadr):4.

21 NT Matthew 1:20; Luke 1:35.

22 NT Matthew 3:16.

23 NT Matthew 12:28; Luke 4:1–2, 14–19; John 3:34.

24 NT John 14–16.

25 NT Acts 1.

26 NT John 14:15–18; 15:26–27; 16:7–15; Acts 1:1–11.

27 Q sura 3 (Al-'Imrân):45.

28 Q sura 4 (Al-Nisâ'):43; sura 5 (Al-Mâ'ida):6.

29 Q sura 19 (Maryam):19.

30 Q sura 3 (Al-'Imrân):46.

31 Q sura 19 (Maryam):31.

32 NT Matthew 8:18–22.

33 OT 2 Samuel 7.

34 OT Psalm 2.

35 OT Psalm 110.

36 OT Micah 5:2.

37 OT Isaiah 7:13–14.

38 OT Isaiah 9:5–6.
39 NT Matthew 1:1; Luke 3:23–31.
40 NT Luke 1:31–33.
41 NT Luke 2:1–7.
42 NT John 1:41, 49.
43 NT Matthew 22:41–46; John 4:26.
44 NT John 6:14–15.
45 NT Matthew 16:13–20.
46 NT Matthew 26:63–64; Mark 14:60–62; Luke 22:66–70.
47 NT John 18:33–37.
48 NT John 19:19.
49 NT Acts 2:36; 13:32–33.
50 NT 1 Corinthians 15:20–28.
51 Q sura 33 (Al-Aḥzâb):40.
52 Q sura 19 (Maryam):30.
53 Q sura 3 (Al-'Imrân):49.
54 Q sura 61 (Al-Ṣaff):6.
55 Q sura 3 (Al-'Imrân):4.
56 Q sura 5 (Al-'Imrân):46.
57 Q sura 19 (Maryam):21.
58 Q sura 19 (Maryam):30–33.
59 Q sura 2 (Al-Baqara):87, 253; sura 3 (Al-'Imrân):49; sura
    5 (Al-Mâ'ida):110; sura 43 (Al-Zukhruf):63; sura 61 (Al-
    Ṣaff):6.
60 Q sura 43 (Al-Zukhruf):59.
61 Q sura 4 (Al-Nisâ'):172.
62 OT Deuteronomy 18:15,18.
63 NT John 1:21.
64 NT John 1:26–27.
65 NT John 6:14.
66 NT John 7:40.
67 NT Matthew 16:14; 21:11; Mark 6:15.
68 NT Matthew 17:5.
69 NT John 5:45–46.
70 NT Acts 3:22; 7:37.
71 NT John 1:45–46; 5:46.
72 NT John 3:17; 4:42.
73 NT John 10:37.
74 NT John 3:34.

75   NT John 17:21, 23.
76   NT John 17:3.
77   NT John 8:42; 17:8.
78   NT John 13:1.
79   NT John 15:13.
80   OT Isaiah 42:1–9.
81   OT Isaiah 49:1–13.
82   OT Isaiah 50:4–11.
83   OT Isaiah 52:13 – 53:12.
84   NT John 1:29.
85   NT Matthew 3:17; 17:5.
86   NT Mark 10:45; Luke 22:27.
87   NT Matthew 26:26–28; Mark 14:24; Luke 22:19–20.
88   NT Matthew 8:16–17; 12:15–21; John 12:37–38.
89   NT Acts 3:13, 26; 4:27, 30; 8:26–35; 13:46–47.
90   NT Romans 5:12–21; 10:16; 15:21; Philippians 2:5–11;
     Hebrews 9:28; 1 Peter 2:20–25.
91   Q sura 3 (Al-'Imrân):45.
92   Q sura 33 (Al-Aḥzâb):69.
93   Q sura 4 (Al-Nisâ'):172.
94   Q sura 3 (Al-'Imrân):45.
95   Q sura 3 (Al-'Imrân):73–74.
96   Q sura 2 (Al-Baqara):253.
97   Q sura 3 (Al-'Imrân):73–74.
98   See R. Arnaldez, *Jésus, fils de Marie, prophète de l'Islam*
     (Paris, Deschée, 1980), ch. X, 'Jesus in Muslim mysticism'.
99   Q sura 72 (Al-Jinn):18, 20.
100 Q sura 6 (Al-An'âm):101; sura 72 (Al-Jinn):3; sura 2
     (Al-Baqara):116; sura 10 (Yûnis):68; sura 17 (Al-Isrâ'):11;
     sura 18 (Al-Kahf):4; sura 19 (Maryam):91–92; sura 21
     (Al-Anbiyâ'):26; sura 25 (Al-Furqân):2; sura 16 (Al-
     Naḥl):57; sura 17 (Al-Isrâ'):40; sura 37 (Al-Sâffât):149–53;
     sura 43 (Al-Zukhruf):19; sura 53 (Al-Najm):27.
101 Q sura 53 (Al-Najm):20.
102 Q sura 19 (Maryam):81; sura 43 (Al-Zukhruf):45.
103 Q sura 43 (Al-Zukhruf):15.
104 Q sura 4 (Ibrâhim):48, 116.
105 Q sura 9 (Al-Tawba):30; sura 19 (Maryam):35.
106 Q sura 5 (Al-Mâ'ida):17, 72.

107   Q sura 5 (Al-A'râf):73; sura 4 (Al-Nisâ'):171.
108   Q sura 5 (Al-Mâ'ida):116.
109   Q sura 4 (Al-Nisâ'):159.
110   Q sura 5 (Al-Mâ'ida):116.
111   Q sura 9 (Al-Tawba):31.
112   NT Matthew 23:8–12.
113   NT Matthew 4:8–10.
114   NT John 8:40.
115   NT John 4:6–8.
116   NT John 11:35.
117   NT Matthew 11:29.
118   NT Mark 10:18.
119   NT John 14:28.
120   NT Mark 13:32.
121   NT John 12:27–28.
122   NT Matthew 3:13–17.
123   NT Matthew 4:17.
124   NT Matthew 7:28–29.
125   NT Mark 2:1–12.
126   NT Luke 7:36–50.
127   NT John 5:19–30.
128   NT John 8:46.
129   NT John 5:18; 10:33.
130   NT John 10:39; 11:53.
131   NT John 12:19.
132   NT John 19:7.
133   NT Matthew 26:63–66; Mark 14:61–64; Luke 22:70–71.
134   NT Luke 5:1–11.
135   NT Matthew 8:27.
136   NT Matthew 11:25–27.
137   NT Matthew 14:33; 16:16; 17:4–5.
138   NT Matthew 5:16,45,48; 6:1,4,6,9,15,18,26,32; John 20:17.
139   NT Matthew 28:18–20.
140   NT John 1:1–14.
141   NT John 16:12–15.
142   NT 2 Corinthians 4:4; Colossians 1:15.
143   NT Matthew 11:27; John 1:18.
144   Q sura 112 (Al-Ikhlâṣ):3.
145   See Chapter 3, note 34.

146   NT Matthew 26:39; Mark 13:32; John 8:40; Acts 2:22; 1 Timothy 2:5.
147   NT Mark 15:34.
148   OT Exodus 4:16; 7:1.
149   OT Psalm 82:6.
150   NT John 10:30–36.
151   NT John 1:12.
152   NT John 17:17–23.
153   NT 1 Corinthians 6:17; 1 John 4:12–15.
154   NT Romans 1:3–4; 8:3,29, 32; 9:5; 1 John 2:22–24; 3:8, 23; 4:9,10,14,15; 5:9–13, 20.
155   NT John 8:56–58.
156   NT John 8:24,28, 58; 13:19; 18:5; also OT Exodus 3:14–16.
157   NT John 14:9–14.
158   NT Matthew 21:33–45.
159   NT John 1:1–18.
160   NT 1 John 4:8 and 16.
161   OT Psalm 103:13.
162   OT Exodus 4:22–23; NT Luke 6:35–36.
163   NT 2 Corinthians 4:4.
164   Q sura 39 (Al-Zumar):4.
165   Q sura 43 (Al-Zukhruf):81.

MUHAMMAD: GOD'S PROPHET?

This question is possibly the most important one for a Muslim, because all the other questions depend on it. Consequently, any in-depth discussion between a Christian and a Muslim leads to this ultimate question: 'We Muslims believe in Jesus, so why don't you Christians believe in Muhammad?' The Christians' attitude seems unjust, incomprehensible, even sectarian. Put in these terms, the question needs elucidation. Certainly Jesus is one of the great prophets of Islam and is revered by all Muslims: but, for Christians, he is much more than a great prophet. He is, as the Gospels testify, the incarnate Son of God.

It is true, however, that some Christians have a negative approach to Islam and to its prophet. I myself have often been shocked and embarrassed by some Christians' hasty judgments on Muhammad, whom they consider as an impostor, a false prophet and even an anti-Christ. Such judgments, far from being inspired by the teaching of Jesus and his apostles, betray a great ignorance of Islam and a lamentable lack of understanding of the biblical doctrine of revelation.

Jesus did indeed warn his disciples that after him would come false prophets and false Christs who would claim to be genuine messengers sent by God. He even predicted that they would enjoy a measure of success, but that their deeds would in the end testify against them.[1] These predictions, alas, soon proved astonishingly accurate as they came true within the lifetime of the apostles. Men who were well-informed about the Christian faith and who had even been members, for a time, of the apostolic communities, began spreading doctrines that were alien to the gospel. As a result, the apostles had to urge Christians firmly to resist these teachings and to expose them as heretical. But the early Christians were also faced with spiritual phenomena for which they were not really prepared; so the apostles told them to examine these things carefully, to hold on to the good and to avoid every kind of evil.[2]

But what of Islam, which appeared some six centuries after Christianity in an area where Christianity was scarcely present and poorly represented? It is not a question of making a value judgment on the religious life of Muslims; only God knows men's hearts! Taken as a whole, Christians probably do not live up to the teachings of the gospel any better than Muslims follow the teaching of the Qur'an. But, when a Muslim asks for an opinion of Islam, it is the Christian's duty to formulate a fair and informed assessment of that religion. The Christian's assessment, on the other hand, must be set in the context of the biblical view of revelation and its specific standards.

GENERAL REVELATION

As the image of God, disfigured by sin but not completely annihilated, mankind possesses a religious sense which enables him to glimpse some aspects of the truth without the help of any revealed religion.[3] In addition to these partial insights into the truth which man can find for himself, God bears witness to himself in the created world, which is 'the work of his hands'.[4] This testimony, though silent, nonetheless displays God's eternal nature, power and glory. This double witness gives every human being a natural knowledge of God independently of any particular self-revelation on God's part. But God also lavishes material and spiritual blessings on mankind without any discrimination.[5] Among the most precious of blessings are the manifestations which God grants to anyone who seeks him.

So the three component parts of God's general revelation are mankind's special status, God's creation, and his universal grace. God's general revelation is the basis on which human beings could reach a genuine knowledge of God if they listen carefully to this threefold testimony. But, in fact, sinful man stifles the voice of his conscience and distorts the witness it bears to God. However sincere man's religious quest may be, it does not prevent him from some form of idolatry, be it subtly or crudely expressed. His awareness of God, however sublime, is consequently limited and, indeed, corrupted.[6] So although the truths contained in natural religions point to the reality of general revelation, this does not mean that God approves of these religions as such.

SPECIAL REVELATION

Since general revelation does not adequately reveal God to mankind, God has taken the initiative of revealing himself directly to us. Out of his sovereign grace he first chose a man, Abraham, and a people, Israel, in order to reveal himself verbally to all peoples of the world. The prophets of Israel were the main witnesses to this revelation. People who were not descended from Abraham also shared in this revelation. From the examples of Job, who lived on the borders of Arabia, probably in the days of the Patriarchs, and of Melchizedek, the Canaanite priest-king whom Abraham knew,[7] we see that God is sovereign and reveals himself to whoever he wishes.

This so-called 'special' revelation was completed by one crowning event 2,000 years ago. Having spoken to mankind through the prophets of Israel, God finally spoke to us through his Son, Jesus Christ, who is the perfect and therefore definitive revelation of God in personal form.[8]

Jesus was fully aware that his mission was the culmination of God's progressive revelation to the people of Israel.[9] Yet he did not hesitate to criticize the conduct of those to whom this revelation had been entrusted,[10] declaring that on the Day of Judgment they would be more severely judged than the people who had not been given the revelation.[11] Nor did Jesus shrink from chiding his own disciples if they simply listened to his teaching without trying to put it into practice.[12] On the other hand, he expressed unreserved admiration for a Roman centurion and a Canaanite woman in whom he saw evidence of faith such as he had not found in any of the people of Israel.[13] He chose to use a Samaritan as an example of neighbourly love when explaining it to a teacher of the Law,[14] and he drew attention to the exemplary behaviour of another Samaritan who had been touched by God's mercy.[15]

So the special revelation enshrined in the Scriptures is the only completely trustworthy basis on which to come to a real knowledge of God. This revelation is therefore the touchstone by which we must measure the truthfulness of all religions, though at the same time we must not anticipate the Last Judgment, which will be faced one day by all mankind.

THE CREDENTIALS OF A PROPHET

We read in the Scriptures that when God sent a prophet to Israel, he was accompanied by signs authenticating his mission. God accredited Jesus in this way by many signs. Because of this great number of signs, Israel's rejection of Jesus was very serious.[16] These signs are important standards by which to evaluate, as necessary, the apostleship of the man whom the Qur'an calls 'the Seal of the Prophets'.[17]

Prophetic predictions

In chapter 6 we saw how the prophecies given by the prophets of Israel concerning, in particular, the new Moses, the Messiah and the Servant of God, were perfectly fulfilled in Jesus. The Qur'an, for its part, maintains that the coming of Muhammad had been foretold by the Scriptures.[18] This, however, is impossible to verify because the Qur'an refers to no biblical texts in support of its statement. Muslim writers, seeking to justify the Qur'anic assertion, have pointed to three passages which are referred to in chapter 3. However, even a brief study of those texts is sufficient to show that they must be predictions, by Isaiah and Moses, of the coming of Christ and the promise, by Jesus himself, of the coming of the Holy Spirit.

Miracles performed

Jesus often confronted those who denied that God had sent him with the fact of his miracles.[19] To those who doubted his messiahship Jesus pointed out that the prophets had spoken of such miracles as signs of the Messiah.[20] But the decisive sign, which Jesus gave to those who continued to reject his apostleship despite his miracles,[21] was that of his resurrection. Jesus spoke of this coming resurrection to his disciples in order to strengthen their wavering faith just before he died.[22] It was to mark the beginning of their full understanding of God's revelation in Christ.

The Qur'an reports no miracles performed by Muhammad, although Muslim traditions attribute many miracles to him. It is, however, extremely difficult to check the historicity of these accounts. In any case, Muhammad did not try to convince his critics by referring to his miracles, but by challenging them to produce a message as perfect in its literary form as the Qur'an which he recited to them.[23] The 'miracle of the Qur'an' seems all the more convincing to Muslims because, according to the Qur'an, Muhammad was 'unlettered'.[24] This term ('*ummi*') has been explained by the Islamic tradition as referring to Muhammad's inability to read or write. But a number of scholars understand it in two other ways.[25] In any case, does the outstanding literary character of a religious book imply its divine origin?

God's testimony

Jesus' baptism marked the beginning of his ministry,[26] his transfiguration was a further revelation to his disciples that he was the Messiah,[27] and his death was the fulfilment of his earthly mission.[28] At each of these important stages God solemnly announced to those present that Jesus was the one he had made responsible for carrying out the plan which he had gradually been revealing to and through the prophets. Even on these few occasions Jesus was presented as the Son of God, unlike any prophet. But God's final testimony to Jesus' status was his resurrection, the truth of which could be attested by more than 500 witnesses.[29] Jesus' apostles claimed to be witnesses of his resurrection[30] and considered that it was unique in history, because in it God supremely revealed Christ's divinity.[31]

According to Muslim tradition, Muhammad was meditating, alone, in a cave near Mecca when the angel Gabriel appeared to him for the first time to reveal the Qur'an to him. Three times Muhammad resisted the heavenly messenger's will that he should recite God's word. Eventually he agreed to receive the first message, which is now enshrined in the ninety-sixth sura of the

Qur'an. This first revelation was followed by many others, which Muhammad received throughout his life. But why were there no witnesses to all these revelations which were collected together into the 114 suras of the Qur'an? It is hard to say. However, it is noticeable that the secrecy of this kind of communication contrasts with the public witness given by God to Jesus. We must also remember that, like all prophets, and like all human beings, Muhammad died awaiting the day of resurrection.

Conformity to God's revelation
Right from the start of his mission, Jesus subjected his preaching to the authority of God's previously revealed word. 'Do not think,' he said, 'that I have come to abolish the Law or the Prophets; I have not come to abolish them but to fulfil them'.[32] Jesus never disputed that God's Law was permanent; indeed, he stressed that the Law must come before human tradition.[33] Jesus' mission was not only to fulfil what had been foretold by the prophets[34] but to bring to perfection the teaching of the Law.[35] Jesus brings out the deep meaning of the Law and so reveals its full implications. Since mankind is incapable of living up to the full demands of the Law, God came in the person of Jesus to raise mankind to the level demanded by the Law. This was the truth revealed by the gospel.

Muhammad also saw his apostolic mission as following directly in the footsteps of his predecessors. The Qur'an confirms the Torah and the gospel but surpasses both of them. Muslims believe that Muslim Law is the definitive Law, in that it reconciles the temporal nature of the Jewish Law with the spiritual nature of the Christian Law. Above all, in the Muslims' view, Islam is the heir to Abraham's religion.[36] Abraham is the father of monotheism because his upright, non-idolatrous surrender to God predates the Laws of Moses and of Jesus.[37] Abraham was therefore neither a Jew nor a Christian but an upright Muslim who had surrendered himself to God,[38] and who, with his son Ishmael, founded the sanctuary at Mecca and prayed that God would send the Arabs a prophet.[39]

Islam was, it is true, the triumph of monotheism over Arab polytheism. Its crowning success was the capitulation of the people of Mecca and the abolition of idolatry in the Ka'ba which, from that time on, became the temple of Islamic monotheism. Islam also presents a coherent body of teaching about God, creation, revelation, mankind, the general resurrection and the Day of Judgment, to mention only the major Qur'anic themes. In their broad outline these themes fit the general framework of Judaeo-Christian revelation.[40] But it must at the very least be said that Qur'anic doctrine knows little of the incarnation of the Son of God, misunderstands the divine Trinity and knows nothing at all of the redemption of mankind by the death and resurrection of Jesus Christ. Muslim theology has explicitly rejected these doctrines, which are central to biblical revelation.

JESUS, MUHAMMAD AND REVELATION

Islam sees itself as summing up earlier revelations and as providing the final revelation from God.[41] Yet when we compare its teachings with those of the Bible, we are forced to question this view of the history of revelation.

The Qur'an embraces, in its own peculiar way, both the biblical tradition and the religious tradition of the Arabs. The guiding principle behind this synthesis is clearly a powerful monotheism rooted in general revelation. But this eminently rational synthesis is nonetheless misleading compared with the special revelation which reached its climax in the person of Jesus Christ, the Son of God. That is why a Christian can subscribe whole-heartedly to the first part of the Islamic creed ('I bear witness that there is no god but God') but cannot, without denying his own faith, endorse the second part ('and that Muhammad is the apostle of God'). This position is the logical outcome of the Christian concept of revelation, just as it is the Qur'anic concept of revelation which leads Muslims to deny that Jesus is the Son of God. This is not to cast doubt on the integrity of Muhammad, who was probably the most zealous Arab of his generation in God's cause.

Do the contrary positions adopted by Christians and Muslims mean, then, that these two groups of people must for ever be opposed to each other? Not at all. Monotheism, which is at the root of both Christianity and Islam, remains the common property of both religions, an inexhaustible source of spiritual enrichment for believers on both sides and a ground on which both sides can meet.

NOTES

1   NT Matthew 7:15–20; Matthew 24:4–5,23–26.
2   NT 1 Thessalonians 5:19–22. Most of the apostolic letters were written to warn early churches against the doctrines of false teachers, which threatened the integrity of the gospel. Some of the letters deal almost exclusively with this problem, particularly Paul's letter to the Galatians and the first letter of John.
3   NT Acts 17:22–29.
4   OT Psalm 8; 19:1–7.
5   NT Matthew 5:44–45; Acts 14:16–17.
6   NT Romans 1:18–23.
7   OT Genesis 14:18–20.
8   NT Romans 9:4–5; Hebrews 1:1–2.
9   NT John 4:4–26.
10 NT Matthew 23:1–36.
11 NT Matthew 10:15; 11:20–24; 12:41–42.

12   NT Matthew 7:21–27; 18:21–35; 25:1–46.

13   NT Matthew 8:5–10; 15:21–28.

14   NT Luke 10:29–37.

15   NT Luke 17:11–19.

16   NT Matthew 11:20–24.

17   Q sura 33 (Al-Aḥzâb):40. Muslim writers explain this title of Muhammad in terms of the two meanings of the verb 'to seal': 'to close' and 'to confirm'. Muhammad is the last of the prophets and he authenticates the message of the prophets who lived before him.

18   Q sura 7 (Al-A'râf):157.

19   NT Matthew 12:22–32; John 10:37–38.

20   NT Matthew 11:2–6; John 10:23–25.

21   NT Matthew 12:37–40.

22   NT John 14:19–20; 16:16–22.

23   Q sura 2 (Al-Baqara):23; sura 10 (Yûnis):38; sura 11 (Hûd):13; sura 17 (Al-Isrâ'):88; sura 52 (Al-Ṭûr):34.

24   Q sura 7 (Al-A'râf):157; sura 29 (Al-'Ankabût):48.

25   The Arabic adjective 'ummi' derives either from the noun 'ummiya' (illiteracy) or 'umma' (nation). If derived from 'ummiya', it would mean that Muhammad was illiterate in the religious sense, i.e. he was ignorant of the Scriptures. See Qur'an, sura 2 (Al-Baqara):78. If derived from 'umma', it would mean that Muhammad was 'unlettered' in the sense that he belonged to those 'nations' which, unlike the 'People of the Book', had not been given a revealed Scripture from God. See Qur'an, sura 3 (Al-'Imrân):20, 75; sura 62 (Al-Jum'à):2. See also K. Cragg, *The Mind of the Qur'an* (George Allen and Unwin Ltd, London, 1973), and *Muhammad and the Christian* (Darton, Longman and Todd, London, 1984), pp. 85–87.

26   NT Matthew 3:13–17.

27   NT Matthew 17:1–8.·

28   NT John 12:20–32.

29   NT John 20:11–29; 1 Corinthians 15:4–8.

30   NT Acts 1:22; 2:32; 3:15; 5:32.

31   NT Acts 2:22–32; 13:32–37; Romans 1:4.

32   NT Matthew 5:17.

33   NT Matthew 5:18–20.

34 NT John 5:46–47.
35 NT Matthew 5:21–48.
36 Q sura 3 (Al-'Imrân):68; sura 22 (Al-Hajj):78.
37 Q sura 2 (Al-Baqara):135; sura 6 (Al-An'âm):79; sura 16 (Al-Naḥl):119.
38 Q sura 3 (Al-'Imrân):65–67.
39 Q sura 2 (Al-Baqara):124–30.
40 These similarities can partly be explained by the Qur'an's literary derivation from the canonical and apocryphal biblical tradition found in Arabia.
41 Q sura 3 (Al-'Imrân):19, 84–85, 109.

PRAYER

Lord,
Let me not become a slaughterer of sheep,
nor a lamb led to the slaughter.
Lord,
Help me to speak the truth before strong men
and not to utter a boastful word
in order to gain the approval of the weak.
Lord,
If you grant me wealth, do not take away my happiness.
If you grant me strength, do not take away my reason.
If you grant me success, do not take away my humility.
If you grant me humility, do not take away my dignity.
Lord,
Help me to see the other side of the situation,
and not to accuse my adversaries of treachery
when they do not have the same opinion as me.
Lord,
Teach me to love others as myself,
and not to demand more of them than of myself.
Lord,
Let not pride overtake me when I succeed,
nor despair overwhelm me when I fail.
But help me always to remember
that failure is the experience that precedes success.
Lord,
Teach me
that forgiveness is the highest expression of strength
and that the desire for revenge
is the worst form of weakness.
Lord,
If you deprive me of money, give me hope.
If you deprive me of success, give me perseverance to overcome
    the failure.
If you deprive me of good health, give me the grace of faith.
Lord,
If I harm anyone,
give me the courage to ask for forgiveness.
If anyone harms me,
give me the courage to forgive.
If I forget you, do not forget me.

Rabindranâth Tagore (translated from Arabic)

POSTSCRIPT

Christianity and Islam. Two distinct religions characterized by faith in one God! This is a hard and painful reality which, on the whole, has not been faced happily by Christians and Muslims. The conflicts in which the two communities have faced each other as enemies down through the centuries bear sad witness to this fact. While sharing a common faith in God, they have, despite themselves, come to share the responsibility of discrediting that faith in the eyes of the world at large. Could they ever humbly admit the wrongs they have done before the God whose mercy they praise, and could they firmly resolve to live together in a new relationship which honours that faith?

The gospel calls Christians — and the Qur'an calls Muslims — to be witnesses for God. It is a call for each of the parties to renounce its comfortable ignorance of the other, to seek to get to know them and accept them as they are. It also involves making the most of the heritage which is common to Christianity and Islam, as well as appreciating the differences, not to mention the contradictions, between the two faiths. God's call awakens in man's heart a love of truth, and this naturally gives an apologetic aspect to a person's witness for God. At the same time, however, he must always respect the other person's conscience and free will.

It was for such purposes as these that this book was

written. My intention was to present the viewpoint of an Arab Christian on a number of theological matters. I must now make it clear that my reasons for writing are not only those that I have mentioned in the course of the book. I wanted, above all, to testify to the wonderful hope which God has brought into my life through Christ, and which his Spirit renews in me day by day, quietly but powerfully. One of the signs of the Holy Spirit's work within me, for which I thank God, is that he has freed me from a long-standing and deep-rooted hostility towards the Jews. May he continue to breathe into me a love for all Jews, Zionists included, equalled only by the love I have for the Palestinian and Lebanese people in this crisis period of Middle-Eastern history.

May we all grow in the knowledge of him whom both Christianity and Islam recognize as our guide and our light!

Also from Lion Publishing:

THE WAY OF JESUS

Dr Bruce Farnham

Many today are curious about the life of Jesus. What is the truth about the stories of his life, his teaching, his death – and rising again? How can we understand them today?

This book is written for the many who simply want to find out about the life and teaching of Jesus, founder of Christianity. The author has lived for many years in the Middle East, and has experienced at first hand both the misunderstandings about Jesus and people's curiosity about who he really was.

Dr Bruce Farnham is a scientist by training. He has written for others who, like himself, live and work in a world which is both increasingly secular and also torn by religious ideologies. It is vital that people from many backgrounds, especially those from other religions, understand the facts and fallacies about the life of Jesus, and how his message is understood today.

More from LION PUBLISHING

LION INTERNATIONAL PAPERBACKS

WHOSE PROMISED LAND? Colin Chapman £3.50 ☐
A detailed study of the Israeli/Palestinian conflict
HEALTH MANUAL:
A SELF-HELP GUIDE Dr Veronica Moss   £3.95 ☐
A comprehensive 'what-to-do' health guide
MADE FOR LOVE Ken Okeke   £2.95 ☐
An examination of the changing pattern of marriage
in Africa
THE WAY OF JESUS Dr Bruce Farnham   £3.95 ☐
(Also available as an 'A' format paperback – priced £2.25
– from March 1988)

All Lion paperbacks are available from your local bookshop or
newsagent, or can be ordered direct from the address below. Just tick
the titles you want and fill in the form.

Name (Block letters) ....

Address ....

....

Write to Lion Publishing, Cash Sales Department, PO Box 11,
Falmouth, Cornwall TR10 9EN, England.

Please enclose a cheque or postal order to the value of the cover price
plus:

UK: 55p for the first book, 22p for the second book and 14p for each
additional book ordered to a maximum charge of £1.75.

OVERSEAS: £1.25 for the first book plus 31p per copy for each
additional book.

BFPO: 55p for the first book, 22p for the second book plus 14p per
copy for the next seven books, thereafter 8p per book.

Lion Publishing reserves the right to show on covers and charge new
retail prices which may differ from those previously advertised in the
text or elsewhere, and to increase postal rates in accordance with the
Post Office.